PRINCESS
to QUEEN

PRINCESS _to_ QUEEN

Catrine Clay

LONDON   NEW YORK   SYDNEY   TORONTO

This book is published to accompany the television programme entitled
Princess to Queen which was first broadcast in April 1996.
The programme was produced by the BBC.
Executive Producer: Eddie Mirzoeff
Producer: Catrine Clay

This edition published by BCA,
by arrangement with BBC Books,
an imprint of BBC Worldwide Publishing.
BBC Worldwide Limited, Woodlands,
80 Wood Lane, London W12 0TT

First published 1996
© Catrine Clay 1996
The moral right of the author has been asserted

CN 8435

Designed by Isobel Gillan
Set in Bembo
Printed in Great Britain by Cambus Litho Ltd, East Kilbride
Bound in Great Britain by Hunter & Foulis Ltd, Edinburgh
Colour separations by Radstock Reproductions Ltd, Midsomer Norton
Jacket printed by Lawrence Allen Ltd, Weston-super-Mare

PICTURE CREDITS

BBC Books would like to thank the following for providing photographs and
for permission to reproduce copyright material. While every effort has been
made to trace and acknowledge all copyright holders, we would like to
apologise should there have been any errors or omissions.

Associated Press 184(t); **Camera Press Limited** 1, 52, 55, 59–61(t), 83,
94(1) Marcus Adams; 163, 181 Baron; 2, 9, 97, 115 Cecil Beaton; 165, 189
Richard Gillard; 3, 119 Karsh of Ottawa; 36, 94(r), 99 ILN; 169 The Times;
129(t); **Tim Graham** 93, 157, 179, 187; **Hulton Deutsch Collection
Limited** 10, 13, 18, 27, 30, 37, 56, 70–73, 76, 78(t), 80, 87, 90–92, 96, 100,
103–107, 111, 112(t) 113, 116–118, 120–123(1), 125, 129(b), 131–136(t),
140, 152–156, 161, 171–176(1), 178, 183, 184(b), 185; **Illustrated London
News Picture Library** 11, 15, 86, 101, 130; **PA News Photo Library**
145(t), 164, 186, 188; **Popperfoto** 25, 28, 39, 44–48, 50, 53, 58, 67, 68, 75,
78(b), 88(1), 98, 109, 123(r), 127, 136(b), 139, 142, 144, 145(b)–148, 151,
162, 167, 177; **The Royal Archives © Her Majesty The Queen** 16, 19,
21, 23, 29, 42, 124 Section of photograph only; 33, 49, 85; **The Royal
Collection © Her Majesty The Queen** 34; **Topham** 61(b)–66, 88(r), 89,
95, 112(b), 126, 149, 159, 168, 176(r).

PAGE 1: *Princess Elizabeth, aged four, with her parents in 1930.*
PAGE 2: *Cecil Beaton's formal photograph of Queen Elizabeth II in her Coronation robes and holding the
Orb and Sceptre – the Sovereign's own regalia.*
PAGE 3: *A portrait study of Princess Elizabeth taken in 1951.*

CONTENTS

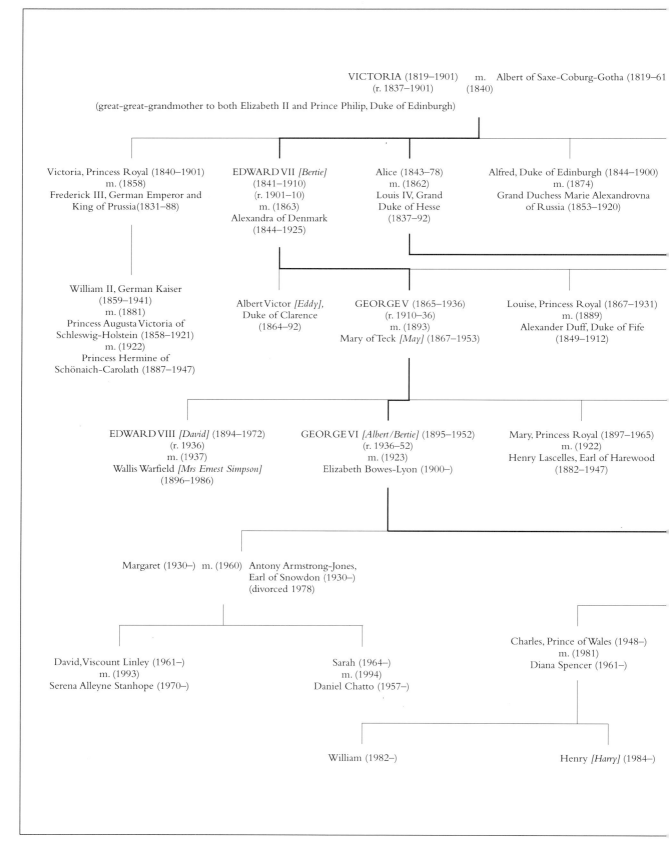

VICTORIA (1819–1901) m. Albert of Saxe-Coburg-Gotha (1819–61
(r. 1837–1901)   (1840)

(great-great-grandmother to both Elizabeth II and Prince Philip, Duke of Edinburgh)

Victoria, Princess Royal (1840–1901)
m. (1858)
Frederick III, German Emperor and
King of Prussia(1831–88)

EDWARD VII [Bertie]
(1841–1910)
(r. 1901–10)
m. (1863)
Alexandra of Denmark
(1844–1925)

Alice (1843–78)
m. (1862)
Louis IV, Grand
Duke of Hesse
(1837–92)

Alfred, Duke of Edinburgh (1844–1900)
m. (1874)
Grand Duchess Marie Alexandrovna
of Russia (1853–1920)

William II, German Kaiser
(1859–1941)
m. (1881)
Princess Augusta Victoria of
Schleswig-Holstein (1858–1921)
m. (1922)
Princess Hermine of
Schönaich-Carolath (1887–1947)

Albert Victor [Eddy],
Duke of Clarence
(1864–92)

GEORGE V (1865–1936)
(r. 1910–36)
m. (1893)
Mary of Teck [May] (1867–1953)

Louise, Princess Royal (1867–1931)
m. (1889)
Alexander Duff, Duke of Fife
(1849–1912)

EDWARD VIII [David] (1894–1972)
(r. 1936)
m. (1937)
Wallis Warfield [Mrs Ernest Simpson]
(1896–1986)

GEORGE VI [Albert/Bertie] (1895–1952)
(r. 1936–52)
m. (1923)
Elizabeth Bowes-Lyon (1900–)

Mary, Princess Royal (1897–1965)
m. (1922)
Henry Lascelles, Earl of Harewood
(1882–1947)

Margaret (1930–) m. (1960) Antony Armstrong-Jones,
Earl of Snowdon (1930–)
(divorced 1978)

Charles, Prince of Wales (1948–)
m. (1981)
Diana Spencer (1961–)

David, Viscount Linley (1961–)
m. (1993)
Serena Alleyne Stanhope (1970–)

Sarah (1964–)
m. (1994)
Daniel Chatto (1957–)

William (1982–)

Henry [Harry] (1984–)

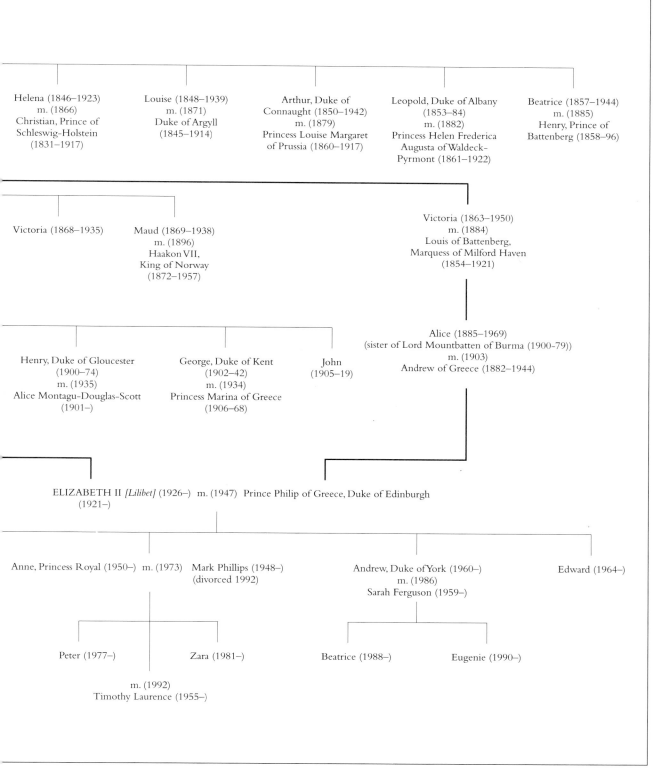

Helena (1846–1923)
m. (1866)
Christian, Prince of
Schleswig-Holstein
(1831–1917)

Louise (1848–1939)
m. (1871)
Duke of Argyll
(1845–1914)

Arthur, Duke of
Connaught (1850–1942)
m. (1879)
Princess Louise Margaret
of Prussia (1860–1917)

Leopold, Duke of Albany
(1853–84)
m. (1882)
Princess Helen Frederica
Augusta of Waldeck-
Pyrmont (1861–1922)

Beatrice (1857–1944)
m. (1885)
Henry, Prince of
Battenberg (1858–96)

Victoria (1868–1935)

Maud (1869–1938)
m. (1896)
Haakon VII,
King of Norway
(1872–1957)

Victoria (1863–1950)
m. (1884)
Louis of Battenberg,
Marquess of Milford Haven
(1854–1921)

Henry, Duke of Gloucester
(1900–74)
m. (1935)
Alice Montagu-Douglas-Scott
(1901–)

George, Duke of Kent
(1902–42)
m. (1934)
Princess Marina of Greece
(1906–68)

John
(1905–19)

Alice (1885–1969)
(sister of Lord Mountbatten of Burma (1900–79))
m. (1903)
Andrew of Greece (1882–1944)

ELIZABETH II *[Lilibet]* (1926–) m. (1947) Prince Philip of Greece, Duke of Edinburgh
(1921–)

Anne, Princess Royal (1950–) m. (1973) Mark Phillips (1948–)
(divorced 1992)

Andrew, Duke of York (1960–)
m. (1986)
Sarah Ferguson (1959–)

Edward (1964–)

Peter (1977–)

Zara (1981–)

Beatrice (1988–)

Eugenie (1990–)

m. (1992)
Timothy Laurence (1955–)

ACKNOWLEDGEMENTS

In writing this book and making this documentary on the Queen's early life, I am indebted to a great many authors who have written biographies of the Queen, or of other members of the Windsor family.

In particular I would like to thank Sarah Bradford, Douglas Keay, Robert Lacey, Elizabeth Longford, John Parker and Philip Ziegler. Their books have been invaluable, but they have also been personally helpful to me, answering queries and discussing various points of interpretation. There is one book, however, which stands out from the rest: the official biography of King George VI, *King George VI, His Life and Reign* by Sir John Wheeler-Bennett, published back in 1958 and used by other authors on royal subjects ever since. When I started writing *Princess to Queen* I found myself increasingly drawn to the close relationship between the father, George VI, and his daughter, Princess Elizabeth. Wheeler-Bennett's superb biography was invaluable. So too was John Pope-Hennessy's biography of Queen Mary, *Queen Mary 1867–1953*. It brought her to life for me – and a very lively person she turns out to be.

Because this book goes hand in hand with the BBC documentary of the same title, I owe equal thanks to the BBC team who have helped me to put the film together. But most of all to Lisa Perkins, my Assistant Producer, who has assisted me unstintingly at every stage and at every level.

Finally, my thanks go to the team at BBC Books who gave me the benefit of their experience, generously and cheerfully.

Catrine Clay

A Cecil Beaton portrait study of Princess Elizabeth in 1948, a year after her marriage.

INTRODUCTION

ABOVE: Princess Elizabeth at her parents' Coronation, aged 11.

LEFT: King George VI and Queen Elizabeth on the balcony of Buckingham Palace after the Coronation on 12th May 1937. The two princesses wear the coronets which their father had specially ordered for them.

One morning in May 1937, a young girl sat down by the window in her schoolroom to write an essay. The schoolroom looked out over the gardens and you could hear the hum of London traffic beyond the garden walls. The girl was just eleven years old. A pleasant average-looking girl with light-brown hair, worn page-boy length with a slide on one side to keep her curls in check. She bent over her lined exercise book in serious concentration and, using a red pencil, she wrote in a clear, neat and rounded hand:

The Coronation, 12 May 1937

To Mummy and Papa. In Memory of Their Coronation, from Lilibet by Herself.

At 5 o'clock in the morning I was woken up by the band of the Royal Marines striking up just outside my window. I leapt out of bed and so did Bobo. We put on dressing gowns and shoes and Bobo made me put on an eiderdown as it was so cold and we crouched in the window looking onto a cold, misty morning. There were already some people in the stands and all the time people were coming to them in a stream with occasional pauses in between. Every now and then we were hopping in and out of bed looking at the bands and the soldiers. At six o'clock Bobo got up and instead of getting up at my usual time I jumped out of bed at half past seven. When I was going to the bathroom I passed the lift as usual, and who should walk out but Miss Daly! I was very pleased to see her. When I dressed I went into the nursery . . .

As an essay it tells us a lot about the eleven-year-old who wrote it. It has the look and feel of an obedient and conscientious child, eager to record the day accurately with attention to detail, and keen to please her parents. There is a charming, rather Victorian use of capital letters. 'To Mummy and Papa. In Memory of Their Coronation. From Lilibet, by Herself.' With these capitals she marks the immense importance of the day, and of her own activity in writing this account of it. It is written by a certain type of eleven-year-old: active, literal, unspoilt, natural. Not dreamy, poetic, eccentric or introverted. She shares her room with Bobo, Margaret MacDonald, the nursemaid. First Lilibet leaps out of bed, then she hops in and out of it. Through her enthusiasm, we can hear the band, feel the cold, see the mist, watch the people 'stream with occasional pauses' into the stands. Finally, at 7.30, she doesn't just get up, she jumps up.

Princess Elizabeth enters Westminster Abbey for the Coronation ceremony. As she greets the Duke of Norfolk she hitches up her Coronation robes – a practical solution, typical of her, to the problem of tripping up.

Miss Daly, whom Lilibet meets coming out of the lift, is her swimming teacher. Lilibet is delighted to see her. Swimming lessons have been the most recent excitement in her life, all the more so because they took place at the Bath Club in Brook Street, Mayfair, with other children in the pool at the same time as Elizabeth and Margaret. This gave the rare and exotic feeling that they were just like other children. Normal children leading normal lives. First they got the Bath Club regulation dark blue swim suits with white initials on them. Then the white bathing caps. Then there were the lessons on a bench when you had to make Y, I, T and X shapes with your arms and legs. Margaret, not yet seven and a bit podgy, kept wobbling. Elizabeth, very much the elder sister, told her 'Keep steady, Margaret!' Their parents often came to watch. 'I don't know how they do it!' said their father, filled with admiration. 'We were always so terribly shy and self-conscious as children. These two don't seem to care.'

And now came the day their father was dreading. The Coronation. The loudspeakers had been tested at three in the morning, waking everyone in Buckingham Palace. By five the band of the Royal Marines was striking up below Lilibet's bedroom window. Her window looked out over the forecourt and right down the Mall. Crowds were gathering there all through the night, singing and shouting. The stands were filling up with thousands of people. 'The whole of London is full of stands for the Coronation,' Queen Mary wrote to her son Edward, by now the Duke of Windsor. 'Too ugly. And the poor daffodils are squashed and hidden underneath.' One wonders what Edward, whose Coronation it should have been, made of this comment. His self-imposed exile, along with Wallis Simpson, the woman he loved, was in a château in the Bois de Boulogne, in France. His younger brother Bertie was the one sitting in Buckingham Palace, trying reluctantly to come to terms with his new position. 'I could eat no breakfast and had a sinking feeling inside,' Bertie wrote later of that fateful morning.

As far as the children were concerned it was all excitement. They raced down to their parents' apartments to show off their Coronation outfits. Both sisters wore long white lace frocks with silver-coloured bows, silver slippers, and cloaks edged with ermine. Their father had asked for two special lightweight coronets to be made for them. Apart from their difference in size, the two princesses looked identical. Their parents liked to see the girls in the same outfits and Elizabeth was

Coronation Day, 12th May 1937. The family of four pose for the official photograph, each looking like a mirror image of the other, only getting smaller and smaller. Princess Margaret wasn't meant to have a train but, being the younger sister, she didn't want to be left out.

> What struck me as being rather odd was that Grannie did not remember much of her own Coronation. I should have thought that it would have stayed in her mind for ever.
>
> At the end the service got rather boring as it was all prayers. Grannie and I were looking to see how many more pages to the end, and we turned one more and then I pointed to the word at the bottom of the page and it said "Finis." We both smiled at each other and turned back to the service

An extract from 'The Coronation' by Princess Elizabeth II, 12th May 1937.

used to it. They didn't approve of discrimination. 'They looked so sweet,' wrote Queen Mary, 'especially when they put on their coronets.'

Elizabeth, as heir presumptive, was to have a short train like her parents. This didn't go down at all well with Margaret. Margaret was a typical younger sister, more lively and less responsible than Elizabeth, and extremely concerned not to be left out. She too wanted a train and made a scene. Her indulgent father gave in. So there they stand in the official Coronation photographs – the four of them, at the very beginning of what the new King, George VI, was to call 'the family firm', each looking like a mirror image of the others, only getting smaller and smaller.

Once the other members of the family arrived, they made their way down to the inner courtyard to the waiting carriages. The horses stamped and snorted. Courtiers, ladies-in-waiting, pages, stewards and footmen were in attendance. The Coronation carriage is a fairy-tale one – all gold and glass and rococo in style. In a ritual which spanned the generations, the family lined up for the procession. There were last-minute adjustments to robes and hair, then through the arch and out into the glare of public life they went. For all the world to see, it was like a magical scene from *Cinderella*.

The two princesses attracted almost more attention than their parents. A machine had been installed on a roof in Whitehall to record the decibels of the roaring crowd – an early example of audience research. It recorded 83 decibels of cheers as the King and Queen's carriage went by. But 85 for the two princesses and their grandmother Queen Mary whose carriage had a specially raised seat in it so that Princess Margaret could see out and be seen. She waved enthusiastically, enjoying every minute.

After the ceremony there was the usual ritual of appearing on the balcony of Buckingham Palace. Here too the photographs tell their own story. In front of Buckingham Palace and all the way down the Mall is thronged with wildly cheering crowds. A sea of faces turned upwards to the family group smiling and waving in return. Queen Mary stands at the centre, with the newly-crowned King and Queen on either side of her. Queen Elizabeth looks the way she will always look from now on in public – gracious and smiling and self-contained. King George VI smiles too. But the worry and anxiety shows through. The two princesses are standing in front of their parents, Elizabeth by their mother, Margaret by their father. They are having fun. They smile and laugh and wave. Princess Elizabeth has a look of near amazement on her face: all those people, all for them.

It was the turning point in all their lives. It was a twist of fate, a hiccup of history, that Bertie stood there and not his brother Edward. Same day, same occasion, different king. No one knew better than Bertie what it meant, now that he was George VI. But could Elizabeth, at 11, understand? Did she realise that nothing would ever be the same ever again?

This is the story of how that 11-year-old girl, a Princess, was trained and schooled from that day on to become Queen of England, Scotland, Northern Ireland and the Dominions – of over 650 million people throughout the world.

CHAPTER ONE

EDWARD AND BERTIE

ABOVE: Edward and Bertie in bathing costumes at Osborne in 1905. The two brothers were close, but very different. Edward was more confident, Bertie was diffident. When he was seven he was forced to write with his right hand despite being left-handed, and he had to wear splints for his knock-knees. He developed a stammer and battled with it for the rest of his life.

LEFT: Bertie and Edward in their prams at York Cottage in 1896. They spent all their childhood together, Edward leading, Bertie following behind. But later on their roles were to be reversed.

The Abdication was a fairy-tale turned sour. A King with the glamour of a Hollywood movie star had given up his throne for the woman he loved. A woman twice divorced, and an American. A woman, then, who would never be allowed to be Queen.

The Royal Proclamation of King Edward VIII had taken place eleven months earlier, on 21st January 1936, the day after George V died, from the balcony of St James's Palace. It was customary for the new King not to be present. But a swift-thinking newscameraman covering the event turned his camera up to a window overlooking the scene. Half-hidden by a curtain stood Edward, forever the one who would do what he wanted to do rather than what was customary. And beside him, just a dark shadow but unmistakable, stood Mrs Simpson.

The funeral of George V took place a week later, on 28th January, at Windsor. It was a State funeral like all State funerals. Solemn and moving. A day when the nation, as a nation, mourns.

George V had died at his beloved Sandringham. 'Am broken-hearted,' Queen Mary wrote in her diary. 'At 5 to 12 my darling husband passed peacefully away – my children were angelic.' The moment he died, Queen Mary turned from her husband who had been King, to her eldest son Edward, who was now King. She stooped and kissed his hand. History had already moved on.

The two princesses, Elizabeth and Margaret, were at Windsor. They'd been sent there from Sandringham a few days before their grandfather died. Now their mother sent a note to Marion Crawford, their governess: 'Don't let all this depress them more than is absolutely necessary, Crawfie. They are so young.'

At nine-and-a-half, Elizabeth was not really quite so young. Before they left Sandringham she was taken by Queen Mary to see her grandfather, and say goodbye. He sat in a chair by the fire in his bedroom, wrapped up in an old Tibetan dressing gown – a relic of one of his visits to India. Who knows what they spoke about, nor if George V, having no illusions about his eldest son, already suspected that this grandchild might one day be Queen? Privately he might even have hoped so. She had always been his favourite. Six years earlier, when he was convalescing from another illness in Bognor, it was Lilibet he wanted to see. She was sent down to stay from London, a chubby three-year-old, with her nurse. She soon cheered him up. 'G. delighted to see her,' Queen Mary recorded in her diary. 'I played with Lilibet in the garden making sand pies.'

A chubby three-year-old, Princess Elizabeth (Lilibet) was sent to Bognor where her grandfather King George V was convalescing. She was always his favourite. 'G. delighted to see her', wrote Queen Mary in her diary.

George V and Queen Mary had five sons and one daughter. Edward, known as David in the family, Albert (later to be known as George VI), Mary, Princess Royal, Henry (later Duke of Gloucester), George (later Duke of Kent) and John who was a sickly child and died at the age of fourteen. All but one were born at York Cottage at Sandringham. They lived in this cramped, dark and extremely unroyal house for thirty-three years, first as the Duke and Duchess of York, then as the Prince and Princess of Wales, and finally as the King and Queen, until Queen Alexandra the Queen Mother, still living in the 'Big House', died.

'It [York Cottage] was, and remains, a glum little villa,' wrote Harold Nicolson in his biography of George V, 'encompassed by thickets of laurel and rhododendron, shadowed by huge Wellingtonians and separated by an abrupt rim of lawn from a pond, at the edge of which a leaden pelican gazes in dejection upon the water-lilies and the bamboos. The local brown stone in which the house was constructed is concealed by rough-cast which in its turn is enlivened by very imitation Tudor beams. The rooms inside ... are indistinguishable from those of any Surbiton or Upper Norwood home ... Against this dismal monochrome hung excellent reproductions of some of the more popular pictures acquired by the Chantrey Bequest ...'

The plumbing was primitive, the children's bedrooms like cubicles. And yet it was home. George V loved it. Queen Mary, ever the dutiful wife, loved it too.

And Queen Mary was certainly dutiful. She had originally been chosen as the wife of Eddy, George V's elder brother (also known as Albert, Duke of Clarence) and the heir to the throne. Eddy had not chosen her. He tended to flit from one unsuitable relationship to another. Queen Victoria, his grandmother, seems, more than anyone, to have chosen her. Princess May (later to become Queen Mary) was the daughter of the Duke and Duchess of Teck – an impoverished and minor branch of the Royal family. Queen Victoria liked them, and housed them in the grace-and-favour White Lodge in Richmond Park. 'We have seen a gt deal of May and Dolly Teck during these 10 days visit here,' wrote Queen Victoria from Balmoral to her daughter Empress Frederick in Germany, '& I cannot say enough good of them. May is a particularly nice girl, so quiet & yet cheerful & so very carefully brought up & so sensible. She is grown very pretty.'

RIGHT BELOW: York Cottage, the modest villa on the Sandringham estate in Norfolk which George V loved more than any other place. RIGHT ABOVE: The Duke and Duchess of York at home in York Cottage in 1895. They lived there for thirty-three years before moving to the 'big house', Sandringham, when they became King and Queen in 1911.

By 19th August 1891, Sir Francis Knollys (the Prince of Wales's Private Secretary) was writing to Sir Henry Ponsonby (Queen Victoria's Private Secretary): 'she [the Queen] came to the conclusion . . . that he should marry Princess May in the Spring . . . I think the preliminaries are now pretty well settled, but do you suppose Princess May will make any resistance? I do not anticipate any real opposition on Prince Eddy's part if he is properly managed.'

She did not make any resistance, and he did not oppose. The wedding was fixed for 27th February 1892. But at Christmas Eddy caught a cold which developed into pneumonia. On 14th January, with Princess May at his side, he died. 'This was an overwhelming misfortune,' Queen Victoria wrote to Sir Henry Ponsonby on the same day. 'One is too much stunned to take it in as yet . . . The poor Parents it is too dreadful for them to think of & the poor young Bride!'

Princess May returned with her parents to White Lodge on 22nd January. In the second week of February, they went to visit Queen Victoria at Osborne. 'The dear girl looks like a crushed flower, but is resigned & quiet & gentle – one is so sad for her,' noted Queen Victoria. May's mother, the Duchess of Teck, wrote to Queen Victoria's daughter, who was the Empress of Germany, 'God is so loving and merciful, one feels there must be a silver lining to the dark cloud, albeit our tear dimmed eyes cannot distinguish it.'

The Duchess of Teck may have been more clear-sighted than she cared to admit. By 29th March Eddy's brother Prince George was writing to Princess May who was in the south of France with her parents. 'Papa and I are coming over to Cannes towards the end of the week for a few days (incog.) and I so hope I shall see you then . . .' Their engagement was announced, after a due period of mourning, on 1st May 1893. A silver lining, indeed, and perhaps a blessing in disguise as well. Where Eddy had been unreliable and volatile, George was straightforward and responsible. Eddy might have been more charming, but George had a stronger sense of duty. He would, in short, make a better King.

The second wedding was arranged for 6th July 1893. In the weeks leading up to it, May and George wrote to each other often. 'I am very sorry that I am still so shy with you,' wrote May, 'I tried not to be so the other day, but alas failed, I was angry with myself! It is so stupid to be so stiff together and really there is

Princess May of Teck at the time of her engagement to George, the Duke of York (later King George V). She had first been engaged to the Duke's elder brother, Eddy. But Eddy died of a sudden illness early in 1892. A year later, encouraged by Queen Victoria, who always favoured her, May agreed to marry George.

nothing I would not tell you, except that I love you more than anybody in the world, and this I cannot tell you myself so I write it to relieve my feelings.' Prince George wrote back the same day: 'Thank God we both understand each other, & I think it really unnecessary for me to tell you how deep my love for you my darling is & I feel it growing stronger and stronger every time I see you; although I may appear shy and cold . . .'

Many years later, when four of their six children had already been born, he wrote to her: 'We suit each other admirably & I thank God every day that he should have brought us together, especially under the tragic circumstances of dear Eddy's death, & people only said I married you out of pity and sympathy. That shows how little the world really knows what it is talking about.'

So this was the royal couple who lived happily in their 'glum little villa' at Sandringham for thirty-three years, bringing up their children, and deferring to George's parents, the Prince and Princess of Wales, who lived in the 'Big House' up the road. Royal life being what it is, there were the routine visits to all the other palaces, and a particular affection for summers spent in Scotland. But Sandringham was always home.

Their three eldest children, Edward, Albert and Mary, were all born within five years. Only eighteen months separated Edward and Albert. They did everything together – Edward leading, Bertie following behind. Royal childhoods are strange childhoods, cut off from other children and surrounded by retainers. Edward and Bertie did the things children do, but they did them alone, cocooned from the rest of the world. Every now and then they were jolted out of their quiet and private lives and thrust into the royal limelight. On 9th August 1902 their grandfather was crowned Edward VII in Westminster Abbey. Edward and Bertie, aged eight and seven, were present. The two princes stood in the Royal box, dressed in their 'Balmoral costume', and watched as their father did homage to his father. As they, in years to come, would do homage to theirs. And as Princess Elizabeth would do homage to hers.

King George V and Queen Mary both loved Edward and Bertie but found it hard to express their feelings. Their father took them shooting and fishing, and taught them drill and how to march up and down on the lawn. Their mother played the piano for them in the evenings. But somehow the stiffness and the

The four generations. Queen Victoria at Prince Edward's (later Edward VIII who abdicated) christening in 1894. Behind them stand the Prince of Wales (later Edward VII) and the Duke of York (later George V).

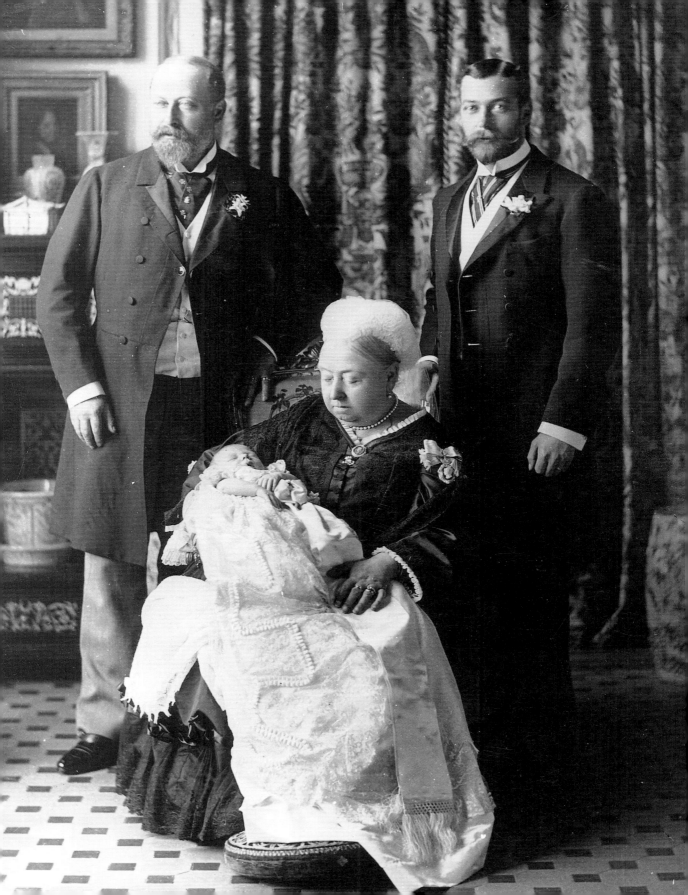

The Prince and Princess of Wales (later King George V and Queen Mary) in India in 1905. From India Prince George wrote crossly to his nine-year-old son Bertie: 'You and Edward seem to have misunderstood that we wanted you both to write to Mama and I every alternate week, as Mary does.'

coolness remained. And always there was the reminder that they were Royal, that one day their father would be King, and that, in his turn, Edward would be too.

'Now that you are five years old,' his father wrote to Bertie, 'I hope you will always try & be obedient & do at once what you are told, as you will find it will come much easier to you the sooner you begin. I always tried to do this when I was your age & found it made me much happier.' When the parents were away for a seven-month State Visit to India, their father sent a cross letter to the nine-year-old Bertie from Delhi. 'You and Edward seem to have misunderstood that we wanted you both to write to Mama & I every alternate week, as Mary does. Edward ought to have written last week instead of this week to me, & you ought to have written to me this week.' To their tutor, Mr Hansell, he wrote: 'The two boys ought to write to the Princess & I each week alternately so that they both write each week.'

Henry Hansell was a forty-two-year-old bachelor who had been in charge of their schooling for the past three years. He meant well, but he was not an inspired teacher and he had some odd ideas. He set up a schoolroom in one of the small, dark rooms at York Cottage, and made Edward Head Boy. It was, and would remain for all their childhood, a class of two. Henry Hansell had a leather-bound Report Book which he filled in assiduously. 'On this, the last page of the second volume of the Report Book [20th May 1905] it will not be out of place if I put down a few observations on the important subject of how the Princes are to be kept up to the mark in their work and in their conduct. A careful survey of the Report Book for each day will show that reports of bad work have been noted and dealt with by me . . .'

The princes were neither particularly clever nor particularly good. They often ended up in their father's study to be lectured to. George V was a naval man, and naval discipline is what he believed in. Edward, always the more cavalier of the two, bore it well enough, though years later he complained that he'd had a miserable childhood. Bertie was frightened and tongue-tied.

Four of King George V and Queen Mary's six children. FROM LEFT TO RIGHT: Henry, Mary, Bertie and Edward with the piper at York Cottage, April 1905. Edward later called it a miserable childhood.

The two brothers were very close, but they were very different. Edward had a superficial ease of manner which his brother lacked. Bertie was naturally diffident. At the age of seven, Bertie developed a stammer which would plague him for the rest of his life. He was left-handed, and at about this time was forced to learn to write with his right hand. The young Albert was also judged to be knock-kneed, so he spent much of his time in splints. With the benefit of hindsight, it is easy enough to see that Bertie was the classic example of a late developer. Contrary to appearances, it was he who would later have the character to take on life's responsibilities, not the apparently more confident Edward. An odd echo of their father George, and his elder brother Eddy.

'This is an experiment!' wrote Bertie from Sandringham to his mother at Marlborough House on 26th February 1904. 'I am sitting in an armchair with my legs in the new splints and on a chair. I have got an invalid table, which is splendid for reading but rather awkward for writing at present. I expect I shall get used to it.' At nine he was already learning forbearance.

In May 1907, when Edward was thirteen, he went to the Royal Naval College at Osborne on the Isle of Wight. He had never been away from home before. 'I felt the parting from you very much,' his father wrote, 'and we all at home miss you greatly. But I saw enough . . . to assure me that you will get on capitally and be very happy with all the other boys. Of course at first it will all seem a bit strange to you but you will soon settle down . . . and have a very jolly time of it.'

At Sandringham, Prince Henry, Edward and Bertie's younger brother, moved up and joined the 'class of two' and Bertie became Head Boy. Mr Hansell reported with his usual flair: 'Last Monday we started seriously on a summer term for our new Schoolroom. Prince Albert is now the Head Boy and Prince Henry has taken the second boy's place. I am very glad to say that Prince Albert gives promise of taking a serious and sensible view of his responsibilities.'

Unfortunately the good start didn't last. The trouble was Bertie's schoolwork, and above all mathematics. He simply couldn't get the hang of it. 'You must really give up losing your temper when you make a mistake in a sum,' wrote his father. 'We all make mistakes sometimes, remember now you are nearly 12 years old & ought no longer to behave like a child of 6.'

The Duke and Duchess of York (later King George V and Queen Mary) with their six children in 1906.
LEFT TO RIGHT: Mary (later Princess Royal), Prince Henry, (later Duke of Gloucester), Prince George (later
Duke of Kent who was killed during the Second World War), Prince Edward (later King Edward VIII and
Duke of Windsor) Prince Albert (later King George VI) and, in his mother's arms, Prince John.

When Bertie was thirteen he followed Edward to the Royal Naval College. Adjusting to life at Osborne had been hard enough for Edward. For Bertie, with his stammer, his difficulty with schoolwork, his shyness, and his virtually total lack of contact with other thirteen-year-old boys, it must have been a nightmare. He was desperately homesick. 'I have quite settled down here now,' he wrote bravely in his first letter home. His father ordered that he be treated like any of the other boys.

The new cadets at Osborne were organised into four groups, and each group had a Term Officer. He was, naturally enough, the most important man on their horizons. Bertie was extremely lucky with his Term Officer. He was in his mid-twenties, a fine athlete and popular with everyone. He was firm but fair. His name was Lieutenant William Phipps, and he turned out to be a friend in need. Bertie was never one to forget a kindness. Years later, when he became George VI, one of the first things he did as King was to appoint William Phipps a Gentleman-Usher-in-Ordinary. Elizabeth, when she became Queen, did the same. She loved her father, and so she loved those he loved.

So it was at Osborne, and at Dartmouth whence Bertie followed Edward two years later, that Bertie first started to show signs of the person he would eventually turn out to be. Equally Edward began to show signs of his developing character. The two brothers were starting on their adult lives.

★　　★　　★

'Went to church after luncheon,' recorded Queen Mary after George V's coffin had been placed in the church at Sandringham. 'It all looked very peaceful – but so sad – My sons returned also Harry & Alice & Elizabeth [her son-in-law and two daughters-in-law]. Did business with Edward who was most helpful and kind.'

On 23rd January 1936, a small funeral procession wound its way from Sandringham to Wolferton station – two long, slow miles. It was a clear winter morning. Forsyth, the King's old piper, played *The Flowers of the Forest*. The coffin rested on a gun carriage. Edward, the new King, walked behind. And a few steps behind him walked Bertie. They looked uncannily alike, both slightly built and both dressed in mourning. But the likeness was an illusion, and their thoughts, as they walked along the Norfolk country road must have been very different.

The two brothers with their father and grandfather: four Kings in one picture. All of them were naval men: Edward and Bertie were both cadets at the Royal Naval College at Osborne on the Isle of Wight.

Frank E. Beresford

When the procession reached the station, the coffin was put on the train. All along the railway track, from Wolferton to Kings Cross, London, groups of people stood to pay their last respects. In London a funeral cortège was formed to carry the coffin, wrapped in the Royal Standard and with the Imperial Crown resting on top, to the Great Hall at Westminster. Edward and Albert, now in the public eye, took up their positions again, the new king in front, the younger brother behind, as they solemnly proceeded through the streets of London, on foot behind the coffin.

Crowds thronged the route: thousands and thousands of ordinary men and women, expressing their national grief. The cortège proceeded to Westminster Great Hall where the coffin lay in state for five days. Four officers of the Brigade of Guards stood at the four corners of the catafalque, heads bowed, hands clasped on the hilt of their drawn swords. Silently, the mourning crowds filed past.

'At midnight my four sons stood guard over their father's coffin for 20 minutes, a v. touching sight,' recorded Queen Mary. Later she commissioned the artist F. Beresford to paint the scene. It was named *The Princes' Vigil* – a title which calls to mind Victorian art and Victorian morality. Queen Mary gave the painting to Edward for his birthday on 23rd June. It is hard to escape from the idea that she was trying to tell him something.

The new king, Edward VIII had reacted strongly, and a little strangely, to his father's death. 'The Prince of Wales became hysterical, cried loudly, and kept embracing the Queen,' recalled Lord Wigram, George V's Private Secretary. George V died at five minutes to midnight. Immediately, Edward made the servants put every clock in the house back half an hour. Back, that is, to real time rather than so-called Sandringham Time. Sandringham Time had been one of his grandfather's quirks, dutifully upheld by his father so that no one would be late.

Change is what Edward wanted. He cut the length of court mourning from one year to six months. As soon as it was over he gave two garden parties for débutantes at Buckingham Palace. Their informality was in strong contrast to his father's old-fashioned court style. 'Signs were not wanting,' Edward wrote years later, 'that many welcomed the advent of my reign as an event of happy augury.'

That summer Edward chartered a yacht and went on a cruise of the Adriatic coast with a small group of personal friends, thus breaking with the established tradition of spending the summer on the grouse moors. Amongst the small group of friends was Mrs Wallis Simpson, the American divorcée. She was certainly a break with tradition, and it was not the last tradition she was about to break.

F. Beresford: The Lying in State of George V: The Princes' Vigil (detail).

CHAPTER TWO

A HAPPY DAY

ABOVE: 17, Bruton Street in Mayfair, the London home of the Strathmores (the Duchess of York's parents) where Princess Elizabeth was born on 21st April 1926. The first bulletin said the Duchess had had a 'certain line of treatment', which was later confirmed as a caesarean.

LEFT: The Duke and Duchess of York with Princess Elizabeth at her christening in May 1926. The gold lily font was brought up from Windsor to the private chapel at Buckingham Palace, and the baby wore the Brussels lace christening gown worn by all royal babies since Queen Victoria.

Princess Elizabeth was born on 21st April 1926 at 17 Bruton Street in Mayfair. It was the London home of the Strathmores, the Duchess of York's parents. Crowds had gathered outside the house in the rain, waiting for news.

'Her Royal Highness the Duchess of York was safely delivered of a Princess at 2.40 am this morning, Wednesday 21st April. Her Royal Highness and the infant Princess are making very satisfactory progress,' announced the Home Office. The first bulletin from 17 Bruton Street referred to 'a certain line of treatment'. The Duchess had had a caesarean.

'We were awakened at 4.00 am by Reggie Seymour [a member of the Royal household],' wrote Queen Mary in her diary at Windsor, 'who informed us that darling Elizabeth had got a daughter at 2.40. Such a relief and joy.' That afternoon the King and Queen motored to London to see the baby. 'We went to London to 17 Bruton Street to congratulate Bertie & we found Celia Strathmore [the Duchess's mother] there, saw the baby who is a little darling with a lovely complexion & pretty fair hair.'

The crowds outside were having a field day. This was Monarchy at its best. Dukes and Duchesses, little fair-haired Princesses, Kings and Queens. All so grand, and yet just like us. Anxious fathers, brave mothers, delighted grandparents.

Bertie was quite overwhelmed. Having seen his mother that day, he wrote to her the next: 'You don't know what a joy it is to Elizabeth and me to have our little girl. We always wanted a child to make our happiness complete, and now that it has at last happened, it seems so wonderful and strange. I am so proud of Elizabeth at this moment after all she has gone through during the last few days, and I am so thankful that everything has happened as it should and so successfully. I do hope you and Papa are as delighted as we are, to have a granddaughter, or would you sooner have had another grandson? I know Elizabeth wanted a daughter. May I say I hope you won't spoil her when she gets a bit older.'

Mrs Clara Knight was to be the nanny. Hers was the old-style of nanny. She always wore uniform and she never talked to the press. She was Mrs, but she never married. She was known as 'Alla' to her charges, a childish version of Clara. Many years before, she had been the Duchess of York's nanny. But if she thought she was going to take full charge of the baby, she was wrong. The Duke and Duchess of York had strong feelings on the matter and they wanted to spend as much time as possible with their children.

The baby Princess Elizabeth with her nanny, Mrs Clara Knight, known as 'Alla'. Riding in a carriage round Hyde Park or Windsor Great Park was always a favourite pastime.

'Elizabeth and I have been thinking over names for our little girl,' wrote Bertie to his father, 'and we should like to call her Elizabeth Alexandra Mary. I hope you will approve of these names, & I am sure there will be no muddle over two Elizabeths in the family. We are so anxious for her first name to be Elizabeth as it is such a nice name & there has been no one of that name in your family for a long time. Elizabeth of York sounds so nice too.'

Choosing names for babies is a very time-consuming matter for all parents. Choosing the name of a Royal baby is even worse.

'I have heard from Bertie about the names,' wrote King George to Queen Mary. 'He mentions Elizabeth Alexandra Mary. I quite approve & will tell him so, he says nothing about Victoria. I hardly think that necessary.'

Even so, the baby princess was already taking her place in history. Named after three queens, it was almost tempting providence.

Her christening took place in the private chapel at Buckingham Palace on 29th May 1926. The 1840 gold lily font was brought up from Windsor, and the baby was dressed in the christening gown of cream Brussels lace worn by all the royal babies since Queen Victoria. The godparents were the King and Queen, Lord Strathmore, Princess Mary, Lady Elphinstone (one of the Duchess of York's sisters) and the Duke of Connaught. 'Of course the poor baby cried,' wrote Queen Mary.

★   ★   ★

Bertie, the late developer, had reached his happiest hour and the happiest stage in his life. He was hardly recognisable as the boy who left Osborne to follow his brother to Dartmouth Royal Naval College. He had passed out of Osborne 68th out of a class of 68. By the time he left Dartmouth he had progressed to 61st out of 67. 'My dear boy this will not do,' his father had written, 'Now remember, everything rests with you, & you are quite intelligent & can do very well if you like. I trust that you will take to heart what I have written ... Our weather here is fine but not as warm as it might and as it ought to be for Ascot ...'

The developing was only just starting. But it was at Osborne that Bertie's saving grace was first spotted. 'He shows the grit and "never say I'm beaten" spirit which is strong in him,' wrote Captain Christian, the Captain of the College, 'it's a grand trait in anybody's character.' Character is what Bertie turned out to have, and character, it seems, is more important than academic qualifications when it comes to being a King. Moreover, although it had taken him a long time to settle down at Osborne, he gradually gained confidence and found, to his own surprise, that he was well liked by the other boys. At Dartmouth it was noted that he never talked 'up' or 'down' to anyone, including the College servants. He was polite and considerate to everyone, whoever they were, and he never gave up.

From January to July 1913, Bertie joined the 9800-ton cruiser HMS *Cumberland* for his final training in foreign waters. He was just seventeen. By now Edward was already embarked on a round of public duties. Their grandfather had died in 1910, and their father was duly crowned on 22nd June 1911. Edward was now the Prince of Wales and not enjoying it much. He described a St John Ambulance Parade as 'rather, if not very dull'. That same day he had to receive the Khedive of Egypt and take the Bishop of Winchester's wife out for dinner. Attending his first Court he noted, 'mighty poor fun ... I went with the parents to the ballroom and stood till 11.00 while hundreds of women went by, each one plainer than the last ... I don't mind if I never go to one again.' Of the State Visit of the King and Queen of Denmark he noted: 'What rot and a waste of time, money and energy all these state visits are.' But these were all comments made privately to his diary. In public he played his part. Shook hands. Smiled. Stood to attention. He was developing into a fluent public speaker.

Bertie's final naval training took him to Trinidad, Porto Rico, Havana, Quebec and St John's, Newfoundland. On 6th June he confided to his diary: 'I was hunted all the time by photographers and also by the Americans who had no manners at all and tried to take photographs all the time.' It was his first real taste of things to come. Wherever they went, balls were given for the cadets. Naturally the seventeen-year-old Prince Albert was the focus of much attention. He was still crippled with shyness and hid away to avoid having to dance but he had begun to grow up, and, when he got home he was no longer tongue-tied in his father's company. 'I am pleased with my boy,' George V wrote to Bertie's Term Officer. He was appointed a Midshipman, and treated, as his father once again insisted, like everyone else. He was known as Mr Johnson and went on manoeuvres in the Mediterranean. By the end of the year in Cairo he was telling his diary: 'We all went to a ball given by Lord Kitchener. I went to bed at 3.00 am having danced nearly every dance.'

But Bertie's real growing up happened during the First World War. 'I got up at 11.45 and kept middle watch until 4.00,' he noted in his diary on 4th September 1914. 'War was declared between us and Germany at 2 am. I turned in again at 4 till 7.15.' Back at Buckingham Palace King George V noted in his diary: 'Please God it may soon be over and that he will protect dear Bertie's life.'

Bertie served on HMS *Collingwood* at the Battle of Jutland. 'It seems curious,' he wrote in May 1916, 'but all sense of danger and everything else goes except the one longing to deal death in every way to the enemy.'

Edward (LEFT) wrote to Bertie: 'I am as good as heartbroken to think I am totally devoid of any job whatsoever and have not the faintest chance of being able to serve my country'. As heir to the throne he wasn't allowed to fight. Bertie (RIGHT) was in France in 1918 where his real growing up took place.

Edward had this to say about the Germans back in 1913: 'The Germans as a race are fat, stolid, unsympathetic, intensely military, and all the men have huge cigars sticking out of their faces at all times.' Now that war had been declared he was appalled to find that, as heir to the throne, he wouldn't be allowed to fight. To Bertie, his closest friend as well as brother, he wrote: 'I am as good as heartbroken to think I am totally devoid of any job whatsoever and have not the faintest chance of being able to serve my country. I have to stay at home with the women and children, a passenger of the worst description!! Here I am at this bloody gt palace, doing absolutely nothing but attend meals . . . However, enough about my rotten self, for I am a most bum specimen of humanity, and so must not be considered.'

This self-hate was a feature of Edward's psychology which turned up again and again in his diaries and his letters to personal friends. And yet, to the outside world, things looked different. He was developing into a regular Prince Charming. His boyish good looks and ease of manner is all the public ever saw. Comparing the two brothers, an unkind contemporary noted: 'It was like comparing an ugly duckling with a cock pheasant.'

After the war, Albert was sent to do a stint at Cambridge University. Edward had done his stint at Oxford. 'I am absolutely fed up with the place and it has got on my nerves,' Edward had confided to his diary. After a lecture on English literature he noted: 'It was very hard to understand and I do not think I shall go to any more.' Mr Hansell's teaching had not prepared either of the boys for this level of education. And they were certainly not intellectuals. But both had remarkable memories, and Edward had a colourful turn of phrase. Predictably, Bertie applied himself more seriously to his studies. He took History, Constitution, Civics and Economics. For a poor mathematician, the latter must have been baffling, but he persevered.

At the same time, Albert was having to take a larger part in public life. The end of the First World War had brought with it a strong interest in Republicanism. The Russian Revolution had swept away the Romanovs. The Imperial thrones of Austria and Germany had also fallen, and Greece looked shaky. In America, President Woodrow Wilson was championing a new world based on greater equality. In England, new ideas of freedom and a fairer society swept the land. The Prime Minister, Lloyd George, promised 'a land fit for heroes to live in', but who were the heroes? The workers wanted a fairer deal from their employers. Mr Bob Williams, Secretary of the Transport Workers Union, was uncompromising. 'I hope to see the Red Flag flying over Buckingham Palace,' he said.

'The Monarchy and its cost will have to be justified in the future in the eyes of a war-torn and hungry proletariat, endowed with a huge preponderance of voting power,' wrote Lord Esher to Lord Stamfordham, the King's Private Secretary.

Canny Lloyd George decided to make a plan. The King's two sons, Edward and Albert, both back from the war, were to fly the flag. Edward by going off on a series of tours of the Empire, Albert by touring the industrial towns of Great Britain. King George V approved both. In the first instance, Albert was to become President of the Boy's Welfare Association, later renamed the Industrial Welfare Society. It was run, with great flair and dedication, by Robert Hyde who had been an East End clergyman. The idea was to improve working conditions, and these conditions should be improved by industry itself, not by government.

Edward, the Prince of Wales, in India in 1922. After the First World War there was a lot of unrest at home, and some threat of Republicanism. Edward was sent off on a series of tours of the Empire, to fly the flag.

Over the next few years, and indeed for the rest of his life, Albert travelled the length and breadth of the country, visiting factories, going down mines, driving trains, meeting dockers, inspecting equipment and talking, always talking, to the workers. He insisted on his visits taking place under normal working conditions. He soon found out for himself how hard the workers' lives were and how much discontent and unrest there was. The workers, for their part, found a man who was genuinely interested in their views, never talked 'up' or 'down' to anyone, and cared deeply.

In this new role, Albert found a cause he could really believe in and a job he could really do. He even made a few, slightly hesitant, speeches. He started to gain a lot of respect and popularity in the country and the public began to refer to him, affectionately, as 'the Industrial Prince.' His brothers called him The Foreman.

With time and experience Albert developed a theory, and this theory he wanted to try and put into practice. It wasn't a complicated theory, but it was full of common sense and it came from the heart. In this, it was typical of the man. Albert felt that a great many of the country's ills stemmed from the simple fact that the boys of the upper classes knew nothing of the boys of the lower classes, and vice versa. It seemed to him that if they could meet, just once in their young lives, on an equal footing, they could find out much about one another. And that this might prevent them, in later life, making sweeping generalisations which were misleading and dangerous. So in 1921 he set up The Duke of York's Camp, which ran for eighteen years, right up to the outbreak of the Second World War.

Each year two boys from each of 100 public schools and two boys from 100 industrial firms were invited to The Duke of York's Camp for one week. The boys had to be between the ages of seventeen and nineteen, and during that week they were to live together, eat together, work and play together. Two from each place were invited because the Duke of York felt that it would help the shy ones amongst them to get over that difficult first day – memories, no doubt, of his own

At home, Bertie formed the Duke of York's camp in 1921 to bring together boys from the upper classes with those from the working classes. It was a scheme close to his heart and it flourished for eighteen years, right up to the Second World War.

shyness as a boy. But the idea was to mix: the Etonian with the Welsh miner, the Harrovian with the Liverpool docker. The team who ran the camps had three principal methods of making sure this would happen. Firstly, on the basis that clothes maketh man, everyone had to change into The Camp's regulation shorts and shirt, so they instantly looked much the same. Then there was the section system which divided the 400 into twenty groups of twenty – each twenty made up of ten from each background. Lastly, all the games they played were competitive, but they were designed to favour the group, not the individual. Loyalty to your section was all that counted in that week.

The Duke of York always visited the camp for one day and it came to be known as 'the Duke's Day'. Wheeler-Bennett, in his biography of George VI, recounts that someone suggested he stay the whole week. Albert refused. 'If I stay you will only be saying every morning: 'What the devil shall we do with him next?' and your own work would be neglected.' He already knew the price of being Royal.

Whilst Albert was making his quiet and unassuming way through the industrial towns of Britain, Edward, the Prince of Wales, was proceeding in a blaze of glory and glamour across the Empire. He was mobbed wherever he went. His natural ease of manner and charm grew by the day. He was blond and blue-eyed, and looked far younger than his twenty-six years. He spoke his speeches fluently and confidently, often without notes. In Canada, he shook so many hands that he had to change to using his left hand. Queen Mary got quite worried about him: 'I feel angry at the amount of handshaking and autograph writing you seem compelled to face . . . this does not sound dignified,' she wrote. To which Edward answered: 'I quite understand what you say about shaking hands and allowing myself to be mobbed & I can assure you that it isn't my fault as you may imagine; you just can't think how enthusiastic the crowds have been . . . one is powerless.'

The real trouble, though, was that Prince Charming didn't feel charming at all. Under the surface brewed the usual dissatisfaction and self-hate. In his three months at home before leaving for his tour of Australia, he wrote to his friend and Private Secretary, Godfrey Thomas: 'A sort of hopelessly lost feeling has come over me and I think I'm going kind of mad!! . . . How I loathe my job now and all this press "puffed" empty "success". I feel I'm through with it and long and long to die . . . Of course I'm going to make a gt effort to pull myself together, and it may only be that I never realised how brain weary I returned from the "Other Side" . . . But my brain has gone and I can hardly think any more.'

It is difficult to know what caused Edward's emotional problems, but one of the symptoms was his fateful attraction to married women, often women who were older than he, and who mothered him or dominated him. First Lady Coke, then Freda Dudley Ward, and, lastly, the divorcée, Mrs Simpson. There were numerous affairs in between, but these were the ones who counted and led, finally and perhaps inevitably, to his abdication.

And it is here, more than anywhere, that the difference between the two brothers showed. Whilst Edward was lurching from one impossible relationship to another, Bertie had met and fallen in love with the most suitable young woman he could possibly have found – Elizabeth Bowes-Lyon.

Elizabeth Bowes-Lyon grew up at Glamis Castle, the ninth of ten children of Lord and Lady Strathmore. It was a happy and secure childhood, full of the life and chatter of a large and united family. Elizabeth was a good friend of Albert's sister, Princess Mary (she had indeed been a bridesmaid at her wedding), so she and Albert were bound to meet sooner or later. This they did at a dance in the summer of 1920. He was twenty-five, she was just twenty. He was still shy and

Glamis Castle, north of Dundee, where Elizabeth Bowes-Lyon grew up. A fairy-tale castle for a girl who was to become an ideal Queen and, later, Queen Mother.

ABOVE: Elizabeth (standing on her mother's left) was the ninth of ten children of Lord and Lady Strathmore. It was a happy and secure childhood. RIGHT: Bertie and Elizabeth on the day of their engagement, 14th January 1923. Elizabeth had taken two years to make up her mind, but Bertie never gave up.

unsure of himself, she was gay and popular. She was dark-haired, pretty and petite. 'The more I see her the more I like her,' Albert wrote to his mother, Queen Mary. He soon decided that Elizabeth was the one he wanted to marry. 'You'll be a lucky fellow if she accepts you,' commented his father, the King.

Elizabeth didn't accept him. She was young and carefree and wanted to stay that way. For two years she fended him off. But Albert applied his usual dogged determination. He had not only found the woman he loved, he had also found a happy family, and he wanted to be part of it. Finally, on 13th January 1923, Elizabeth said yes. Albert instantly wrote a telegram to his parents: 'All right. Bertie,' is all it said. The Court Circular of 16th January formally announced the betrothal and stated that 'The King has gladly given his consent'.

'Elizabeth is charming, so pretty & engaging & natural. Bertie is supremely happy,' wrote Queen Mary in her diary. Pretty, engaging and natural. Three excellent attributes for a future Queen. She was strong too. And this, as both

Bertie   *Jan. 14th 1923*   *Elizabeth*

ABOVE: The official wedding photograph, 20th April 1923. This was the turning point in Albert's life. From then on Elizabeth stood firmly by his side, and he steadily gained in self-confidence. BELOW: The Duke and Duchess leave for their honeymoon in an atmosphere of great happiness. The two brothers exchange a private smile before the carriage goes through the gates of Buckingham Palace and into the glare of public life.

parents knew, was what Bertie needed. From that day on, Albert, the late developer, started to gain confidence and come into his own. 'You & Papa were both so charming to me yesterday about my engagement,' he wrote to his mother in a letter which hums with happiness, '& I can never really thank you properly for giving your consent to it. I am very very happy & I can only hope that Elizabeth feels the same as I do. I know I am very lucky to have won her over at last.'

Elizabeth and Albert were married in Westminster Abbey on 26th April 1923. It was the wedding of the decade. Crowds camped outside Buckingham Palace all through the night and thronged the route to the Abbey to catch a glimpse of the bride. *The Times* wrote: 'There is but one wedding to which the people look forward with still deeper interest – the wedding which will give a wife to the Heir to the Throne and, in the course of nature, a future Queen to England and the British peoples.' Edward, the Prince of Wales, was by this time already embarked on his great affair with the married Freda Dudley Ward. As he stood beside his brother Albert in Westminster Abbey waiting for Elizabeth Bowes-Lyon to come up the aisle, he must have felt a deal less confident than *The Times* about the prospect of his own marriage.

'Dear Bertie,' wrote George V, 'You are indeed a lucky man to have such a charming & delightful wife as Elizabeth & I am sure you will both be very happy together & I trust you both will have many many years of happiness before you & that you will be as happy as Mama and I are after you have been married for 30 years, I can't wish you more. . . . You have always been so sensible & easy to work with & you have always been ready to listen to any advice & to agree with my opinions about people & things, that I feel that we have always got on very well together (very different to dear David) . . . By your quiet useful work you have endeared yrself to the people, as shown on Thursday by the splendid reception they gave you. I am quite certain that Elizabeth will be a splendid partner in your work & share with you & help you in all you have to do.
Wishing you & Elizabeth every good luck & a very happy honeymoon.
Ever my dear boy
Yr. most devoted Papa'

★   ★   ★

So, now, three years later, the Duke stood beside the gold lily font, watching his first daughter being christened. It was one of the happiest days of his life. 'We always wanted a child to make our happiness complete.' As yet, there was no premonition that this simple happiness wouldn't last for ever.

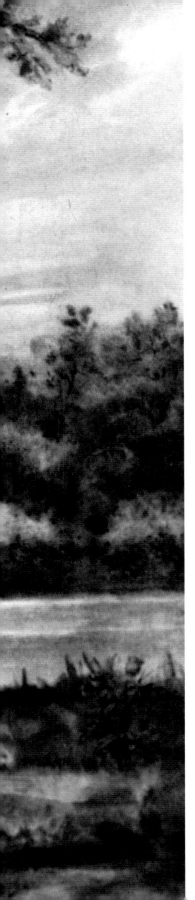

CHAPTER THREE

THE FOUR OF US

ABOVE: Margaret and Elizabeth, 1932.

LEFT: The two princesses were not only photographed – patiently they posed for paintings at all stages in their childhood.

In spite of their best intentions, the Duke and Duchess of York had to leave their baby daughter for six months when she was nine months old. On 6th January 1927 they sailed aboard HMS *Renown* from Southampton for a tour of the Antipodes and to open the Australian Parliament in the new capital of Canberra. Royal duty was royal duty, and Albert would have been the last person to demur. Baby Elizabeth was left in the care of Alla and her grandparents. 'I quite felt it, leaving on Thursday,' wrote the Duchess to Queen Mary, 'the baby was so sweet, playing with the buttons on Bertie's uniform, that it quite broke me up.'

The tour was an ordeal for Albert. He was there to represent the King and it would be a non-stop round of public engagements which he always found something of a strain. Worst of all, there would have to be many speeches. Albert's stammer was still a problem, and when he got tired or nervous it got much worse. However, he had his young wife beside him. She seemed able to charm everyone, and she gave him constant support.

A year earlier the Duchess had persuaded her husband to see Mr Lionel Logue, a speech therapist. Mr Logue had a practice in Harley Street, and Albert started to go there four or five times a week. His wife often went with him. Without her he would probably have given up, the problem was so difficult and too dis-heartening. But it turned out that Mr Logue was able to make a difference. He told the Duke two important things. Firstly, that the secret to public speaking lay in breathing correctly and taking his time. And secondly, that the real secret lay in the patient's own mental attitude. The only person who could cure his stammer, Mr Logue pointed out, was the Duke himself.

On the tour, Albert sometimes had to make three speeches a day. It was a tremendous strain, but the earlier sessions with Mr Logue helped. So did the crowds who gave the Duke and Duchess an ecstatic welcome wherever they went. There was something about this young and rather modest couple which appealed to them and caught their imagination. The Duke's stammer wasn't cured, but it was lessening. And for the first time, he started to believe that he could beat it. On the steps outside Parliament House, he made a speech which was all his own idea.

'It is impossible not to be moved by the significance of today's events as a landmark in the story of Australia,' he said, taking a careful breath. 'I say this not only because this day sees the opening of a new Parliament House and marks the

Princess Elizabeth on her first birthday, 21st April 1927, posing with her proud grandmother, Queen Mary. Her parents were away on a six-month tour of Australia and New Zealand.

Princess Elizabeth, aged 3, and Alla at King's Cross station, setting off for Christmas with the grandparents at Sandringham.

inauguration of a new Capital City – but more because one feels the stirring of a new birth, of quickened national activity, of a fuller consciousness of your destiny as one of the great self-governing units of the British Empire.

'Today marks the end of an epoch and the beginning of another, and one's thoughts turn instinctively to what the future may have in store. One's own life would hardly be worth living without its dreams of better things, and the life of a nation without such dreams of a better and larger future would be poor indeed.'

This, surely, is the unmistakable voice of Albert, the struggling young man who dreamed of better things, and was at last seeing some of them fulfilled.

'His Royal Highness has touched people profoundly by his youth, his simplicity and natural bearing. . . . The visit has done untold good and has certainly put back the clock of disunion and disloyalty 25 years as far as this State is concerned,' wrote Lieutenant-General Sir Tom Bridges, the Governor of South Australia, to George V.

THE FOUR OF US

There was huge interest in Princess Elizabeth. Three whole tons of toys were given to the Duke and Duchess for her before their return. 'It is extraordinary how her arrival is so popular out here. Wherever we go cheers are given for her as well & the children write to us about her,' Albert wrote to his mother back home. 'I am glad to be able to give you the most excellent accounts of your sweet little daughter, who is growing daily,' wrote King George V. 'She has 4 teeth now, which is good at 11 months old, she is very happy and drives in a carriage every afternoon, which amuses her.'

George V may have been a difficult father, but he was an ideal grandfather. Riding in carriages is just what small children like to do, and he was more than happy to oblige. He was a man of regular habits too. Breakfast was always at 9 o'clock sharp. You could set your clock by it. Before that the King would already have done some hours of work on his state papers. He'd come in to the breakfast room at Buckingham Palace or Sandringham, followed by a couple of his terriers and with Charlotte, his parrot, perched on his finger. Charlotte would hop onto the breakfast table and have a good look round. Sheer joy for a child.

It was George V who started to call Elizabeth Lilibet, the only way the child could say her own name. Soon enough the whole family was using it. 'I am so glad little Elizabeth is behaving herself so well with you,' wrote Albert, adding somewhat anxiously, 'I do hope you will not spoil her too much, as I have always been told grandfathers are apt to.'

When the Duke and Duchess came home on 27th June, the streets were lined with cheering crowds welcoming them back. The press had reported their successes, and the Duke and his 'dainty Duchess' were fast becoming a favourite at home as well as abroad. In front of Buckingham Palace, the place was packed with people as George V, Queen Mary and the Duke and Duchess of York came out onto the balcony. Best of all, the Duchess had Princess Elizabeth in her arms. Queen Mary held an umbrella over them to keep off the rain. Albert looked happy. George V looked pleased. The baby, Princess Elizabeth, looked surprised to be held by this stranger who was her mother.

It was Princess Elizabeth's first appearance on the balcony of Buckingham Palace, her first performance on the royal stage, but she already had a starring part. The papers were full of pictures and stories about her and the crowds craned their necks to catch a glimpse. That balcony is just like a stage, with all the players taking their part. The show had started for Princess Elizabeth, and it turned out to be the longest-running show in town.

Princess Elizabeth with her parents and grandparents on the balcony of Buckingham Palace, 27th June 1927. Her parents had been away on tour for six months, returning home to a tumultuous welcome.

The family moved in to 145 Piccadilly, their first London home. It was a stone's throw from Buckingham Palace which suited the grandparents very well since they were by now very attached to the baby and wanted to see her as much as possible. The house was later bombed in the war, but in those days Hamilton Gardens lay behind the house, surrounded by railings with a gate which led in to Hyde Park beyond. It was a large London house, but not particularly grand. The Duke and Duchess were both keen to lead as normal a life as possible. The nurseries were on the top floor. They were light and airy, and Alla reigned supreme.

The following May, George V appointed Albert to be Lord High Commissioner of the General Assembly of the Church of Scotland. It was a great honour and a mark of George V's growing confidence in his second son, for Albert was to represent the King in Scotland. He and the Duchess of York went up to Edinburgh and took up residence, as a formality, in Holyrood House on 20th May 1928.

Princess Elizabeth aged two years three months, with her mother at an early 'photo-opportunity'. Public interest in the little princess was high from the start. Her dress, her bonnet, her hair and her very blue eyes.

ABOVE: *Princess Elizabeth, aged three, with her parents at another photographic session. The Duke and Duchess of York were given toys for the princess wherever they went. They brought back three tons of toys from the Australian tour.*

LEFT: *Princess Elizabeth, aged two. Here she stands in her best dress looking sturdy and serious.*

BELOW: *The night nursery at 145 Piccadilly where the York family moved when the Princess was a year old.*

'The only thing I regret is that we have not got Lilibet here,' the Duchess wrote to Queen Mary. 'I fear that it has been a very great disappointment to the people. Not that they would have seen her, but they would have liked to feel that she was here. In the solemn old Assembly, the Moderator mentioned in his welcoming address "our dear Princess Elizabeth", which is, I believe, almost unique. It almost frightens me that the people should love her so much. I suppose that it is a good thing, and I hope that she will be worthy of it, poor little darling.'

Luckily the 'poor little darling' did not have to go on bearing the weight of all that adulation alone. On 21st August 1930 Princess Elizabeth got a baby sister. She was born at Glamis, and she was named Margaret Rose. They had wanted to call her Ann Margaret, but George V didn't like the name Ann, so her parents settled for Margaret Rose instead. Now there was someone else to share the nurseries on the top floor of 145 Piccadilly, and Lilibet was pleased. The landing outside her bedroom was lined with toy horses which she groomed every night. It was a lot of work and an extra pair of hands would come in useful.

In 1931, George V gave the Duke and Duchess of York Royal Lodge in Windsor Great Park for their country house. They added new wings and painted it pink. The garden was large and Albert set about taming it and planting his beloved rhododendrons. Year by year it became more of a home, and more of a retreat from the increasingly public life they had to lead in London.

In 1932, Miss Marion Crawford joined their household. She was twenty-three, a Scottish girl with an independent air and some progressive views. She had trained at the Moray House Teacher's Training College in Edinburgh. She had always wanted to teach, but never intended becoming a governess. Her interest lay with the poor. However, a living had to be earned, and by 1932 she was back home in Dunfermline walking many miles a day across the hills to teach the children of some of the local aristocratic families. Amongst these were the children of the Duchess of York's elder sister, Lady Rose. It was there that she met the Duke and Duchess of York, who had come in search of a governess for Princess Elizabeth, now nearly six. They liked her at once. Marion Crawford was full of energy and she had a lively mind. She was young and she was fun. Just the sort of person they were looking for. The Duke, with his memories of his own poor education under Mr Hansell, was delighted. Miss Crawford was employed for a trial period of one month. She stayed for seventeen years.

Princess Margaret, aged three and Princess Elizabeth, aged seven in 1933. Princess Elizabeth, proud of her gloves and special handbag, poses patiently for yet another photograph.

A routine was soon established. The mornings were taken up with lessons. Then there was elevenses. Before lunch there was a time for reading with one or other parent. Miss Crawford found that Princess Elizabeth could already read, and that anything involving dogs or horses was always a safe bet. Down at Royal Lodge, 'Crawfie', as she was soon to be known, always had lunch with the Duke and Duchess and Lilibet. Margaret, round-faced and chubby, would join them from the nursery at the end of the meal just in time to get some of the brown sugar her father was putting into his coffee. The afternoons were taken up with lighter activities: dancing lessons, singing, painting. King George and Queen Mary came to inspect the new governess. The King wanted to make sure the children were taught a good handwriting. Queen Mary wanted to make some alterations to the timetable. Not enough History and Geography, she thought, for children who were, after all, royal. For her fourth birthday, Queen Mary had given Lilibet a set of building blocks made from fifty different woods coming from fifty different parts of the Empire. The grandmother, chosen by Queen Victoria to become Queen herself, was determined that her grandchild should know who she was.

These five years before the turmoil of the Abdication were very happy ones for the York family. Crawfie noted how much time the Duke and Duchess managed to spend with their children. Every morning started with the girls coming down to their parents' rooms to talk and play. Tea-time was often followed by a session of Racing Demon, Snap or Happy Families. Every night was bath night, with a lot of laughing and splashing about. And after that came the pillow-fights. The Duchess may have been following her own childhood rituals. The Duke was making up for lost time.

It was very much 'the four of us', as the Duke liked to say. Sometimes there were guests at tea or in the evenings. But often the family was alone. Some of the most charming photographs date from this time. They walk together, they garden together, they sit and listen to the wireless together. Much like any other family in Britain at the time. Only they weren't like any other family, and as time went on, they became so less and less.

Typical of this split was the way the two girls were brought up. Both parents wanted them to have as normal an upbringing as possible. Yet in those days it wasn't possible for them, as royals, to go to a normal school. Their contact with

Elizabeth and Margaret spent most of their childhood in each other's company – with few other children around, they became great playmates.

other children of their own age was limited and worse still, right from the start other children treated them differently. Their closest relationships were, in fact, with their retainers – Crawfie, Alla, Owen the groom who looked after their ponies, and Bobo, the railway worker's daughter from Scotland who helped Alla, and now slept in Lilibet's room. Without wanting it, the Princesses were forced to live in a world of their own.

The two girls spent most of their childhood in each other's company, with Lilibet early on adopting the role of keeping her sister in order. There was a four-year gap between them, which made it quite clear who was boss. But even without the gap, Lilibet's character was sensible and straightforward whereas Margaret's was more wayward and contrary, so they fell easily into their respective roles.

RIGHT: The two sisters at their other grandparents' (Lord and Lady Strathmore) home in 1932.

BELOW: The two princesses in 1933 with their groom Owen. Owen became, for some time, the most important person in Princess Elizabeth's life.

There they are, in all the newsreel footage and all the photographs, the two princesses, side by side and always dressed in identical outfits. Elizabeth, taller and more serious looking. Margaret, the younger one, often grinning at the camera.

Their parents, in those early days, spent many evenings on their own together. The Duchess liked jigsaws and cards. The Duke liked to do needlepoint. Queen Mary had taught all her children to stitch. It was just one of the many surprises in store for Mrs Simpson as she got to know Edward better.

The Prince of Wales was living a life very different from the domestic and bourgeois life of the Yorks. As the 1920s progressed into the 1930s he looked and acted more and more the eternal bachelor. He had his affairs, went constantly to Mayfair nightclubs, and generally spent his time with the kind of people disapproved of by the King and Queen. The gap between his public image and his private life grew more and more difficult to bridge. From about 1926 onwards he cared noticeably less about his work. 'I'm fed up with princing,' he complained. This had always been so, but now it was starting to show.

In 1931, Edward met Wallis Simpson. In retrospect, it was a passion just waiting to happen. The man who wanted to subject himself wholly and abjectly to one woman, and the dominating woman who wanted worldly wealth and position above all else. Once it had started, no one could stop it. Not even for a throne. By 1934 Mrs Simpson had dispatched any rivals and she reigned supreme. If she dropped a hairpin on the floor, Edward went on his hands and knees to pick it up for her. He showered her with jewellery from Cartier's which cost a fortune. Worse still, Edward showered her with family jewels which had been left to him by his grandmother, Queen Alexandra, for his future wife. When Wallis was away Edward was miserable. When she was there, he had eyes for no one but her. Lady Diana Cooper, an old friend, recalled that Mrs Simpson might tear her nail. Edward would jump up instantly. 'He needs must disappear and arrive back in two minutes, panting, with two little emery boards for her to file the offending nail.'

In November 1934, Prince George, the fourth son of King George V and Queen Mary, married Princess Marina of Greece. Princess Elizabeth, now aged eight, was a bridesmaid. There was a ball given at Buckingham Palace to celebrate the wedding, and on his list of guests Edward included the name of Mrs Ernest Simpson. George V, without a word, crossed it out. Edward put it back. Mrs Simpson came and Edward introduced her briefly to his mother. Not to his father.

Princess Elizabeth, aged eight, accompanying her grandparents, King George V and Queen Mary, to Westminster Abbey to a service for the unemployed.

'That woman in my own house!' King George stormed later. It was a clear sign that Edward wanted acceptance and recognition for Mrs Simpson. And a clear sign that he was completely out of touch. Mrs Simpson, about to be divorced a second time, could never have acceptance or recognition.

The Prince of Wales saw less and less of his family. The two princesses found that their favourite uncle rarely dropped in for tea and a game of Snap any more, and if he did, he was distracted. In public he often looked bored or irritated. There were rumours that he was impressed by the Nazis in Germany. Mrs Simpson went to dinner at the German Embassy. By 1935 his Private Secretaries were seriously worried. So was Mr Baldwin, the Prime Minister, and the Government. Edward was becoming unpunctual. He sometimes cancelled engagements, if there was a chance he could see Mrs Simpson. It was becoming almost impossible to keep the scandal out of the papers.

Lady Airlie, one of the King and Queen's closest friends, wrote in her book, *Thatched With Gold*, that by 1935 King George V knew the score. 'I pray to God my eldest son will never marry and have children,' he said, 'and that nothing will come between Bertie and Lilibet and the throne.'

In May 1935, it was George V's Silver Jubilee. There was a great procession of royal carriages to St Paul's Cathedral, the King and Queen in the first and the Prince of Wales, his thoughts no doubt elsewhere, in the next. The Yorks, with the two princesses in identical rosebud-pink outfits, followed in the third carriage. The whole route was thronged with wildly cheering crowds. During the Thanksgiving service in St Paul's, the two princesses, now nine and five, sat on two stools directly behind the two thrones of their grandparents. Later that day the whole family went out onto the balcony of Buckingham Palace to wave to the huge crowd assembled below. The people cheered and cheered. They wanted an encore. Every night that week they came and they cheered. 'I had no idea they felt like that about me,' said King George, genuinely surprised.

By Christmas, the King was seriously ill. On Christmas Day, he broadcast to the Nation and the Empire for the last time. 'It is this personal link between me and my people which I value more than I can say.' His voice sounded thin. 'It binds us together in all our joys and sorrows.' By 20th January, he was dead.

On the balcony of Buckingham Palace for King George V's Silver Jubilee, May 1935.

CHAPTER FOUR

THE TURNING POINT

ABOVE: Princess Elizabeth in 1937.

LEFT: On Friday, 11th December 1936 Edward VIII made his famous Abdication speech. Then he left for France to join Wallis Simpson. 'Best love and best luck to you both' he wrote to Bertie and Elizabeth from France.

Nineteen-thirty-six was the year of three Kings – George V, Edward VIII and George VI. Edward VIII was proclaimed King on 21st January, the day after his father died. His Coronation was planned for 12th May of the following year. But on 11th December he abdicated, and on the following day Albert, his brother, was proclaimed King. Albert chose the name George, thus illustrating once again the fundamental difference between the two brothers— Edward rejecting everything his father had stood for, Albert accepting it, and continuing with it. Continuity is one of the things monarchy can offer a nation. Without it, monarchy is nothing. Edward, with his inability to understand this, had put the monarchy in jeopardy. His brother, George VI, would set it back on course.

The countdown to the Abdication reads like a thriller. No one could know the outcome till the very last minute – perhaps not even the chief protagonists. More and more people turned up at 145 Piccadilly to discuss the events with the Duke and Duchess of York. Private Secretaries, members of the Cabinet, Archbishops, and finally Baldwin, the Prime Minister, himself. As summer gave way to autumn, and autumn to winter, the visits became more and more frequent, and more and more tense.

The two princesses, now ten and six, watched all the comings and goings from the top of the stairwell and tried to work out what it all meant. They were used to important people coming to the house. Their father's royal duties required plenty of meetings and he had kept up his active interest in industry, still working hard for the Industrial Welfare Society. Trade Unionists and top industrialists were frequent visitors. But these new people were different. And the mood of their visits was different too – serious and hushed. The princesses also noticed that their parents looked more and more strained. By the end of November their mother was in bed with 'flu, and their father looked sick with worry.

That summer, Edward had refused to do the usual rounds of royal residences and went on a cruise instead. Mrs Simpson went with him. At Sandringham, his father's beloved home, Edward instigated sweeping economies calling it a 'voracious white elephant'. At Buckingham Palace, in a similar drive to slim down the expenses of monarchy, he cut the servants' beer money. Unfortunately the King also used the servants to deliver crates of champagne to Mrs Simpson, now installed in an apartment in Regents Park.

Edward VIII and Wallis Simpson on a cruise during the summer of 1936. Usually Royal summers were spent at Balmoral. Edward was breaking all the rules.

When Edward arrived at Balmoral for two weeks, it was with a house party of his own friends, not the usual mix of dignitaries and archbishops. He cancelled a visit to an Aberdeen hospital, saying he was still in mourning. The Duke of York went instead and it later transpired that Edward had been otherwise engaged, picking Mrs Simpson up from the station. The Yorks were staying at Birkhall nearby. The Duchess only agreed to visit Balmoral because her husband insisted. Mrs Simpson was acting as hostess, and she was training the kitchen staff to make double decker all-American sandwiches. It was hard to bear.

Queen Mary must have watched the developments with a sinking heart. She knew how her husband had felt about their eldest son, and although she had always been more indulgent, she knew he was right. But there was nothing she could do. Typically, perhaps, Queen Mary decided to pretend nothing was wrong. When Edward had the clocks at Sandringham put back to their proper time, even though his father had only just died, she declared it an excellent idea. When he halved the length of Court mourning, she agreed with that too. When he didn't go to church, although now, as King, he was Head of the Church, she turned a blind eye. When he came back from his summer cruise, she was delighted to see him. 'David (Edward) came back from abroad looking very well and came to dine with me and we had a nice talk,' she wrote in her diary on 14th September.

Queen Mary busied herself moving out of Buckingham Palace and in to Marlborough House. 'To Marlborough House at 10.25 and stayed there till after 1 — supervising various things and arranging furniture — Went there again at 3 and stayed till 7.30!!! I took my tea there and had it with Mrs Moore our housekeeper, picnic fashion in one of the rooms — Felt dead tired on my return,' she wrote in her diary that September. On 1st October she left Buckingham Palace for the last time. On her first evening in Marlborough House she bravely wrote, 'I think I shall be quite contented here tho' there must always be the fearful blank.'

During the same month, Mrs Simpson started divorce proceedings against her second husband, Ernest Simpson. He did the decent thing, offering himself as the guilty party though the case was plainly the other way round. Baldwin went to see the King. Sir Alexander Hardinge, Edward's Private Secretary, paid a visit to 145 Piccadilly. What Hardinge and the Duke of York discussed is not recorded,

Princess Elizabeth and Princess Margaret, aged nine and five, pose for a photograph in the garden of Royal Lodge, Windsor, with their mother and dogs in the summer of 1936. Royal Lodge was the family's country retreat, and the large garden gave the King plenty of scope to indulge in his favourite hobby — cultivating rhododendrons.

but it is not difficult to imagine. On 13th November, with Baldwin's agreement, Alexander Hardinge sent a letter to the King. He explained that the press, so far extraordinarily discreet, could no longer be relied on to hold their silence. The Government did not like the situation and might resign. Then there would be a General Election. Hardinge begged his Majesty to send Mrs Simpson abroad, without further delay.

The letter was a turning point for Edward, but not in the way Hardinge anticipated. On 16th November, he asked Baldwin to call on him at Buckingham Palace. He told Baldwin he intended to marry Mrs Simpson and abdicate if necessary. That evening Edward went to dine with his mother. 'To my mother the Monarchy was something sacred and the Sovereign a personage apart,' Edward wrote many years later of that evening. 'The word "duty" fell between us.'

It was eighteen months before Queen Mary really spoke her mind. In July 1938, she wrote to her eldest son Edward, who was now the Duke of Windsor, living in France with the woman he loved: 'You will remember how miserable I was when you informed me of your intended marriage and abdication and how I implored you not to do so for our sake and for the sake of the country. You did not seem able to take in any point of view but your own ... I do not think you have ever realised the shock, which the attitude you took up caused your family and the whole Nation. It seemed inconceivable to those who had made such sacrifices during the war that you, as their King, refused a lesser sacrifice ... My feelings for you as your mother remain the same, and our being parted and the cause of it, grieve me beyond words. After all, all my life I have put my country before everything else, and I simply cannot change now.'

Queen Mary, who, as Mary of Teck, had agreed to marry first one brother, then the next, simply could not understand or forgive Edward. She turned her attention to Albert, her second son. It was a case of history repeating itself – the younger brother once again taking over from the elder.

LEFT ABOVE: *Princess Elizabeth, aged eight, outside her Wendy House, 'The Little Welsh House', in the grounds of Royal Lodge in June 1936. It was a gift from the people of Wales, and fully furnished, just like a real house.*

LEFT BELOW: *The Royal Family at the 'Little House'. Bertie and Elizabeth attached a great deal of importance to family life and made a special effort to bring up their two daughters in as normal an atmosphere as possible. The whole family adored their dogs and spending time with them was one of their greatest pleasures.*

Albert was feeling more and more dismayed. He, too, could hardly believe that Edward would really do this, and the outcome for himself and his family was almost unimaginable. He felt completely unprepared for the task – he was just a naval officer. He had never seen a state paper in his life, he said. Moreover, he knew better than anyone that he had none of his brother's natural flair. He was still shy, and he still stuttered when he was tired or anxious.

At 145 Piccadilly it was decided that the two princesses needed something to distract them from the growing tensions. It was Marion Crawford, now into her fifth year as their governess, who had the idea of swimming lessons. Elizabeth and Margaret were longing to do what other children did, and no doubt begged and pleaded with their parents. 'The Duke and Duchess were wonderfully good about allowing these innovations,' noted Crawfie later, 'though some of the older members of the family, I fear, did not always approve.' In the event, the princesses

Princess Elizabeth, aged ten, in her swimming team. Life was to go on as usual, even though behind the scenes the Abdication was unfolding.

were allowed to go to an ordinary swimming pool, with ordinary children, and have ordinary swimming lessons like anyone else. 'On our first trip Alla made preparations of such magnitude that we might all have been going out on a raft to a desert island. Large bath towels, dusting powder, combs and brushes, a small box of chocolates were all packed up into quite a large zip bag. I think had she had her way she would have added a couple of life-buoys.' The swimming teacher, Miss Daly, wondered whether she should curtsey to the two princesses. When they had an hour to spare, the Duke and Duchess liked to come and watch. It was wonderful relaxation from a situation which was getting worse by the day.

On 3rd December the press broke its silence. Albert tried again and again to see Edward but Edward kept putting him off. It took five days. On Monday, 7th December, Albert later recorded in his diary: 'My brother rang me up at ten minutes to 7.0pm to say "Come & see me after dinner," I said "No, I will come & see you at once." I was with him at 7.0pm. The awful & ghastly suspense was over. I found him pacing up & down the room & he told me his decision that he would go.'

Three days later, the Duke went to see his mother. 'I went to see Queen Mary & when I told her what had happened I broke down & sobbed like a child,' he wrote in his diary. She, for her part, wrote in hers: 'It is a terrible blow to us all and particularly to poor Bertie.'

In his book *Monarchy*, Robert Lacey points out an intriguing gap. Edward had told Baldwin of his decision to abdicate on 5th December. Albert wasn't told until 7th December. 'The best explanation,' Lacey writes, 'would seem to lie in the widespread fear in December 1936 that Prince Albert, Duke of York, was not capable of taking over the throne as the successor of his elder brother.' In theory it would have been possible to skip a brother and crown the Duke of Kent instead. He already had a young son (the present Duke of Kent) who could become Prince of Wales. Sir John Wheeler-Bennett, in his official biography of George VI, indignantly writes of the rumours current at the time: 'There was the crowning calumny that, even if he succeeded in getting through the ordeal of the Coronation, the King would never be able to undertake all the arduous duties which would fall to him, that he would never be able to speak in public, and that he would be a recluse, or, at best, a "rubber stamp".'

In the event, George VI was neither a recluse, nor just a 'rubber stamp'. He turned out to be one of the most loved and respected monarchs the country had ever known. But the strain of it never went away. The call of duty was strong in him but in the end made him ill, and most probably led to his early death.

On Thursday, 10th December, Albert drove back to 145 Piccadilly from Windsor. 'I later went to London where I found a large crowd outside my house cheering madly. I was overwhelmed,' he wrote. The two princesses now knew that something serious was going on. Elizabeth, aged ten, probably had a good idea what it was, though certainly not what it meant. The Duchess of York was still in bed with the 'flu and she called Marion Crawford to her room.

'The Duchess was lying in bed, propped up among pillows,' Marion Crawford recalled. 'She held her hand out to me. "I'm afraid there are going to be great changes in our lives, Crawfie," she said. We talked for a little while as to how we were going to break this news to the children, and what differences it would make. The break was bound to be a painful one. We had all been so happy in our life at 145.

On Friday, 11th December, Edward made his now famous Abdication speech, and Albert became King George VI. The following day Edward boarded the destroyer HMS *Fury* at Portsmouth and set sail for France. Albert attended his Accession Council at St James's Palace and addressed, for the first time, his Privy Counsellors. He looked pale and exhausted. He was more nervous than he need have been, because he too had heard the rumours about his unsuitability for the job. He fell back on dogged determination, and addressed the Privy Counsellors clearly, but with many hesitations. His first act as King was to confer the new Dukedom of Windsor on his brother Edward.

Later that day, Edward telegraphed Albert from France. 'Glad to hear this morning's ceremony went off so well. Hope Elizabeth better. Best love and best of luck to you both.' What Albert and Elizabeth thought of that is not recorded.

First of all they had to leave 145 Piccadilly, where they had been so happy, and move into Buckingham Palace. Children rarely like change, and the two princesses were shocked. Marion Crawford was horrified. 'People think that a royal palace is the last word in up-to-date luxury, replete with everything the heart could desire, and that people who live there do so in absolute comfort. Nothing could be farther from the truth. Life in a palace rather resembles camping in a museum. These historic places are so old, so tied up with tradition, that they are mostly dropping to bits, all the equipment there decades behind the times.' It wasn't homely. 'We felt it was all far too big. It was five minutes' walk to get out into the gardens. Whichever way you went, there were those interminable corridors . . . On my first morning at the Palace, when I crossed the corridor on the way to my bathroom, it was a shock to run into a postman . . .'

All through her childhood Princess Elizabeth had corgis. She even took one – Susan – on honeymoon with her.

Against all predictions, and his own fears, King George handled the Coronation ceremony on 12th May 1937 with great dignity. Indeed it must have been something of a revelation to him to find that many around him were more nervous than he was. 'My Lord Great Chamberlain was supposed to dress me,' he noted that same evening in his diary, 'but I found his hands fumbled & shook so I had to fix the belt of the sword myself.' The Archbishop seemed unsure which way round to place the St Edward's Crown. One of the Bishops trod on the King's robe when he was leaving the Coronation Chair, so that Albert nearly tripped.

The two princesses, wearing their Coronation robes and special coronets, sat beside their grandmother in the royal box, and watched as their parents were crowned. The King had given Elizabeth a specially-bound volume of the Coronation Service to study beforehand. Queen Mary had produced a thirty-foot coloured panorama of George IV's Coronation for the two princesses some weeks earlier. Continuity being the hallmark of monarchy, very little had changed since 1821. There were the Bishops, the Peers and Peeresses and the Pages. There were the numerous relations from all the Royal families of Europe. There was the ritual, and there was the pageantry.

'Bertie & E looked so well when they came in & did it all too beautifully,' recorded Queen Mary that evening in her diary. 'The service was wonderful & impressive – we were all much moved . . .' She must have thought back to her own and George V's Coronation. And beside her stood the eleven-year-old Elizabeth, the heir presumptive, looking serious and responsible, carefully reading her service book.

'Grannie and I were looking to see how many more pages to the end,' wrote Elizabeth in her essay, 'and we turned one more and then I pointed to the word at the bottom of the page and it said "Finis". We both smiled at each other and turned back to the service. . . . When we got back to our dressing-room we had some sandwiches, stuffed rolls, orangeade and lemonade.'

The crowds which thronged the Coronation route cheered until they were hoarse. If ever Albert had a doubt that he was the right man for the job, it must have been dispelled on that day. The King and Queen were called out again and again onto the balcony of Buckingham Palace. Watching the Movietone newsreel of that occasion now, sixty years later, it is astonishing to see how strongly the crowd felt about them. 'We want the King! We want the King!' they keep shouting, their great mass of laughing and smiling faces turned up to that one family, smiling and waving back at them. And out onto the balcony they come again, Queen Mary taking it all in her stride. The rest of them looking delighted, touched and amazed in turns.

Coronation day Bertie & Elizabeth.

Dull day, & rain - 12 WEDNESDAY (132—233) & I left
at 10.10. for Westminster Abbey in
glass coach, escort of Horse guards.
Crowds everywhere, most enthusiastic.
Arrived 10.55 - Maud & I processed
up the Abbey to the Royal Box.
I sat between Maud & Lilibet, &
Margaret came next. they looked too
sweet in their lace dresses & robes,
especially when they put on their
coronets. Bertie & E. looked so
well when they came in &
did it all too beautifully.
The Service was wonderful &
impressive - We were all
much moved. It was over by 1.45.
We then walked to our room where
we had something to eat & joined
B. & E. in their room. The long drive
to Buck. P. started at 2.25.; I going
with the 2. children, we had a
marvellous reception. B. & E. arrived
about 4. We all went out on the
Balcony - great reception - Were then
photographed - got back at 6.30.
a wonderful day -

An entry from Queen Mary's diary for 12th May 1937, the Coronation of her second son.

ABOVE: *On 2nd June 1953 Elizabeth II was crowned Queen of England, Scotland, Northern Ireland and the Dominions. Queen of 650 million people. She was just twenty-seven years old.*

LEFT: *Bertie was crowned King George VI on 12th May 1937. Against all predictions and his own doubts he turned out to be one of the best-loved and most respected monarchs.*

LEFT: *Princess Elizabeth, aged six with her corgis. When Marion Crawford first became the princesses' governess, she soon found that any books on dogs or horses were an instant hit.*

RIGHT: *Princess Elizabeth proudly cycling in Hyde Park on her tricycle. In the pram is the baby Princess Margaret.*

OPPOSITE: *Elizabeth and Margaret at the piano. Both princesses took lessons and liked, on occasion, to play duets.*

During the dreadful previous December, James Maxton, a Labour MP, had proposed to replace the Crown with a republican system. He was defeated in the House of Commons by 403 votes to 5. The reception the crowd gave their new Royal family that day proved that the country felt the same.

The psychology of monarchy is a fascinating study. What must it feel like to receive that kind of adulation? How to cope with the constant attention of the press? Ever since Elizabeth was born, the newspapers had been full of pictures of the little princess – in her new yellow bonnet, with her favourite corgi dog, or at her piano lessons. Overnight, yellow bonnets were a sell-out, everyone wanted corgis, and daughters all had to have piano lessons.

*Princess Elizabeth on her thirteenth birthday riding in the grounds at Windsor with her father
and sister. They all shared a love of horses.*

Perhaps in reaction, the King and Queen were even more determined that their daughters should be brought up simply. There was the annual outing to a pantomime and the Royal Tournament, the occasional film show, plenty of home family entertainment like charades and cards, and quiet family holidays in Scotland and Sandringham. At Christmas the princesses wrote excited letters to Santa Claus, and neat thank you letters afterwards whilst Lilibet made lists to remember who gave her what. The girls loved riding, dancing reels and doing jigsaws. Aged ten, Princess Elizabeth went to bed at 7.15, half an hour later than Margaret. When she was thirteen, she was still dressed in identical dresses and white socks as her sister who was nine.

Life at Buckingham Palace was certainly grander than at 145 Piccadilly. The rooms were huge, the corridors endless and there were footmen everywhere. But Lilibet and Margaret soon got used to it, and the place began to feel a lot more cheerful with the sound of children's laughter filling the empty rooms. But Marion Crawford recalls seeing Elizabeth looking wistfully out of the window at a boy speeding past Buckingham Palace on his bicycle. She was longing for a bicycle, and possibly for more freedom too.

Occasionally the two girls had to appear in public. Garden parties were particularly hard work. The princesses trailed behind their parents, smiling and shaking people politely by the hand, getting hot and tired. The irrepressible Marion Crawford says she found it more convenient to watch the proceedings from her room, through a pair of field glasses. She recalls Elizabeth telling Margaret one day, 'If you do see someone in a funny hat, Margaret, you must NOT point at it and laugh.' She was ever the elder sister.

But Elizabeth was now heir presumptive and that, in a small way at first, made a subtle difference to the relationship between the two sisters. But then increasingly, Elizabeth started to be trained to one day take over from her father and become Queen. In April 1937, when she was eleven, Elizabeth performed her first public duty beside her father. Together they took the march past of the Boy Scouts at Windsor. Boy Scouts, Trooping the Colour, Passing Out Parade at Sandhurst, Flypasts, Inspection of the Fleet – all these duties and engagements require much the same of the Sovereign, and this was the first taste of what much of the rest of Elizabeth's public life would hold. She was learning her new job.

22nd December 1937. The King and Queen, accompanied by Princess Elizabeth and Princess Margaret, on their way to Sandringham for Christmas.

ABOVE: The Queen at the Trooping the Colour ceremony, 17th June 1995. As Princess Elizabeth she attended Trooping the Colour (LEFT) many times. Here, in 1938, she leaves Buckingham Palace with her sister and Queen Mary. Her own first Trooping was forty-five years ago in 1951, taking the place of her father who was ill.

LEFT: Princess Elizabeth aged twelve. Soon her lessons in the history of the British Constitution would begin. RIGHT: An unofficial trip with Crawfie on the Underground. These trips were less tiring and more fun than the official trips which were made with Queen Mary. OPPOSITE: When George VI and Queen Elizabeth departed for a six-month tour in 1939, the two princesses saw them off with Queen Mary and other members of the family.

Queen Mary now stepped up her educational trips with her two granddaughters. The Wallace Collection, the Tower of London, Hampton Court, the British Museum, Kew Gardens – they visited them all and at length. Queen Mary's energy in the cause of duty was great, but not necessarily shared by the two princesses. It was left to Marion Crawford to take them on their first exciting trip on the Underground.

In May 1939, the King and Queen went off for a tour of Canada and the United States. Queen Mary and the two princesses went down to Portsmouth to see them off. 'The ship left punctually at 3,' she wrote that evening in her diary. 'It was a fine sight from the jetty – & we waved handkerchiefs. Margaret said "I have my handkerchief" & Lilibet ansd. "To wave, not to cry" – which I thought charming.' Margaret may not have found it quite so charming. But it shows that Lilibet was very much a chip off the old block.

When the King came back from that tour, he was a changed man. The trip had been an overwhelming success. Everywhere the new Monarch and his Queen were mobbed by cheering crowds. The King's speeches went well and he no longer felt in his brother's shadow. 'There must be no more high-hat business,' he said to one of his advisers. 'The sort of thing that my father and those of his day regarded as essential as the correct attitude – the feeling that certain things could not be done.' The man who had put so much effort into the Industrial Welfare Society and who had brought public schoolboy and factory worker together at his Duke of York Camps was now setting his own agenda. The King liked the more classless society he saw in America and Canada, and he wanted some of it for Britain. After meetings he now always made his own notes. He insisted on reading all his letters before, not after, his Private Secretary. The casual legacy left by his brother was banished for ever.

That summer the family went on a cruise up the River Dart on the Royal Yacht, *Victoria and Albert*. They stopped to visit the Royal Naval College at Dartmouth, where George VI had once been a cadet. It is recorded as the first time Princess Elizabeth met another naval cadet – Philip Mountbatten. She was thirteen and he was just eighteen. But by now, war was only months away.

CHAPTER FIVE

THE WAR
YEARS

ABOVE: Princess Elizabeth on her sixteenth birthday.

*LEFT: When Buckingham Palace was bombed in 1940, Queen Elizabeth
said, 'I'm glad we've been bombed. It makes me feel I can look the East
End in the face.'*

In September 1939 the Nazis crossed the border into Poland, and Britain was at war. Along with every other family in the land, the Royal family had to decide what to do. Should they stay in London, at Buckingham Palace? Should they go to the country, out of the way of the bombs? Should they send the two girls to Canada? What should Queen Mary do?

Queen Elizabeth seems to have settled a large part of it. She made an official statement: 'The children won't leave without me; I won't leave without the King; and the King will never leave.' As Douglas Keay says in his book *Elizabeth II, Portrait of a Monarch*, you could almost hear the cheers.

It was decided that Elizabeth and Margaret should stay at Windsor. For the first six months they had been in Scotland and at Sandringham, but these were so far away, and the separation, for all of them, was too hard to bear. The medieval walls

RIGHT: The Royal Family sitting on a wall at Royal Lodge. 'The four of us', as the King liked to say. Family life was to remain as normal as possible, even though father and mother were King and Queen.

BELOW: Windsor Castle, home for the two princesses for the duration of the Second World War, safe from the London Blitz.

of Windsor were considered thick enough to be bomb-proof. As an additional precaution, they dug some trenches and put up some barbed wire. 'The feeble barbed wire of course wouldn't have kept anybody out but it kept us in,' Princess Margaret later recalled. An official photograph of the two princesses was duly released to the press. They were seated in a pony cart, smiling at the camera, with one of the corgis perched between them. The caption read 'taken in the garden of the country residence where they are staying during the war.' No one should know their whereabouts.

The King and Queen spent the weekends at Windsor, but most of the week in London at Buckingham Palace. Every night, at six, they rang their children. As the war progressed, they went about their daily business undeterred. They visited hospitals, heavily-bombed areas, munitions factories and troops. They made

RIGHT: During the week George VI and Queen Elizabeth were up in London visiting hospitals, heavily bombed areas, munitions factories and air-raid shelters. BELOW: 'Taken in the garden of the country residence where they are staying during the war.' Thus read the caption to this official photograph. It was important that no one knew of their whereabouts.

speeches, presented awards, entertained Ambassadors, Bishops, and Chiefs from the Armed Forces. Together with the rest of the country they worked for war and they prayed for peace. When Buckingham Palace was bombed in 1940, Queen Elizabeth was almost pleased. 'I'm glad we've been bombed. It makes me feel I can look the East End in the face,' she said.

Various Royal refugees who were fleeing the Nazis turned up at Buckingham Palace. They all set to, sending out food parcels, organising sewing and knitting mornings, and replying to the hundreds of letters received.

Queen Mary, now aged seventy-two, decided she should leave Marlborough House and go to the country. Her niece, May, was married to the Duke of Beaufort and they lived at Badminton, in Gloucestershire. Badminton is a very fine country house set in its own extensive parkland. It dates from the seventeenth and eighteenth centuries and is filled with beautiful pictures and furniture. Just Queen Mary's cup of tea. Her niece invited her to stay and she was accepted. On the day Queen Mary arrived, the Duchess of Beaufort was a little alarmed to see so many black cars coming down the drive. Queen Mary arrived with sixty-three servants. She stayed for six years.

She chose a nice suite of rooms for herself on the first floor looking out over the parkland. She had brought with her some favourite pieces and ornaments – the rest being stored at Windsor. All this was very pleasant and Aunt and niece got on well. But Queen Mary was restless. The fact of the matter is, she was a city person. At Sandringham or Balmoral she might take a walk round the gardens or the estates, but she had no country pursuits. What should she do all day?

At first Queen Mary would spend at least one day of each week in London, leaving early in the morning by train, and coming back exhausted in the evenings. She'd pop in to Marlborough House, go to exhibitions, have lunch at Buckingham Palace with the King and Queen, and perhaps see her dentist or doctor. 'London looks very warlike,' she noted after one visit, 'sandbags, ARP men with tin helmets & gas masks, Police ditto – windows boarded up etc.' It was the so-called phoney war, before the real bombing started.

Back at Badminton, Queen Mary did a lot of needlework, re-read all her diaries and wrote many letters. She also set to work sorting out papers – a favourite pastime. She liked tidiness. Luckily the Beaufort papers and documents, reaching back hundreds of years, were in a bit of a mess. She made her way through them all, reading them carefully and putting them into envelopes which she signed and

King George VI in uniform at Buckingham Palace in 1940. Like his father and grandfather before him, George VI was a naval man.

dated. Years later the family were looking for a document to prove that John of Gaunt had granted their ancestors some rights concerning the River Severn. Sure enough, there they were, in their envelope, signed Mary R, 1940.

In addition there were the evacuees from Birmingham living in the village, and the 120 men of the Gloucestershire Regiment billeted in the Badminton stables. All these people could be visited and encouraged, as could the local hospitals and factories. But the best solution of all was the ivy, which Queen Mary loathed. She set about clearing the entire estate of this vile creeper – it was her own personal war. She, her lady-in-waiting, her equerry, and a couple of her despatch riders would set forth with some sturdy gardening tools to tidy things up. 'Lovely morning which we spent clearing ivy off trees,' she wrote happily in her diary. 'We watched a whole wall of ivy of 50 years standing at the back of Mary B's bedroom being removed – most of it came down like a blanket.' One hopes Mary B felt the same way about the ivy.

In the meantime, the two princesses were settling in to the routine of life at Windsor. It wasn't very exciting, for Windsor in wartime was a bleak place, with all the paintings, precious objects and chandeliers removed. They saw much less of their parents now, and spent most of their time with Marion Crawford, Alla, and Bobo. They did their lessons, played the piano, went riding, they knitted for the war effort, they gardened in their allotments. One of the more exciting developments was that they restarted their Girl Guide company which they had originally formed at Buckingham Palace. At the Palace it had consisted exclusively of the daughters of Palace staff and Royal relations. Consequently, there was always an element of artificiality. But now the company was made up of the village children and some evacuees from the East End of London. They were real Cockneys and they weren't bothered that the two girls were Princesses. For once, Elizabeth and Margaret were part of normal life.

Nights were often spent in the air-raid shelter, down in the dungeons. 'Who IS this Hitler, spoiling everything?' Margaret, aged nine, asked Crawfie. Often, the princesses sat by the wireless to hear the latest news. The wireless was central to their lives, as it was to everyone else at that time. Both princesses loved Tommy Handley and *It's That Man Again*, and *Much Binding In The Marsh*. When they heard Lord Haw Haw preaching his Nazi propaganda they used to throw books and cushions at the wireless. On the wall they had a large map with flags pinned on it, to follow the progress of the war.

At Windsor the two princesses got on with their normal lives in relative safety. Every morning they took lessons.

ABOVE: *Royal Lodge, Windsor, April 1940. Like everyone else during the war, the two princesses had their allotments and did their gardening.*

LEFT: *The two princesses sitting on the lawn at Windsor Castle with Jane, a favourite corgi. The parents liked to see their daughters dressed the same, even though, by 1941, Princess Elizabeth was fifteen years old.*

When war broke out, Princess Elizabeth was thirteen. By the time it was over she was nineteen. Her growing-up was done in wartime, a time of black-outs, air-raid warnings and family disruption. It was not a carefree time. There was always an underlying anxiety – most of all about their parents who spent their time in London, even during the Blitz. 'Do you think the Germans will come and get them?' a worried Margaret asked. She was always a child with a vivid imagination, and her dreams were often lurid. On the other hand, from her point of view it was quite a realistic fear. Their family stories were full of coups and assassinations.

When Elizabeth turned thirteen, she started to take lessons in the history of the British Constitution with Sir Henry Marten who was Vice-Provost of Eton. It was another step in her gradual training for her future role as Queen. In the beginning Marion Crawford took Princess Elizabeth to Sir Henry's study at Eton but as the war became more threatening, he came twice a week to Windsor Castle. Elizabeth at first felt shy and quite overwhelmed by the amount of books lying in great piles in Sir Henry's study. She was used to reading *The Children's Newspaper* and *Punch*, but this was something quite different. 'Crawfie, do you mean to tell me he has read them ALL?' she asked in some disbelief. She had never known a scholar before. However, Sir Henry turned out to be charming and broadminded. 'Like a book to read Miss Crawford?' he asked Marion Crawford who sat in a window-seat and waited while Elizabeth had her lesson. And he handed her the latest P. G. Wodehouse.

Thirteen is not very old to start applying your mind to the ins and outs of the British Constitution. But Elizabeth was a serious thirteen-year-old, keen to learn and keen, above all, to please her parents. She was quite reserved, but this came partly from her over-protected childhood. There was none of the nerviness in her which dogged her father throughout his public life. Elizabeth already had her feet firmly planted on the ground. The King and Queen knew all this, and they felt she was ready to start her training. It was only a matter of finding the right teacher, and in Sir Henry they had that. By the time she was fifteen Princess Elizabeth knew more about the history of the British Constitution than most of us do in our entire lives.

A further step in her training came on 13th October 1940. It was her first broadcast. Elizabeth was fourteen, and that broadcast, like all the others which were to come, was listened to by millions across the nation and the Empire. She spoke on the BBC's *Children's Hour*, introduced by the famous Uncle Mac. It was one of her and Margaret's favourite programmes on the wireless, and now here she was, with Margaret at her side, taking part.

'This is the BBC Home Service. Hello children, everywhere,' Uncle Mac began in his usual way. He went on, somewhat reverently: 'Today Princess Elizabeth is herself to take part in the *Children's Hour* and speak to the children of the Empire at home and overseas. Children in the United States of America will also hear this broadcast. Her Royal Highness, Princess Elizabeth.'

And then you hear her voice. She starts a little high and a little fast, sounding much younger than her fourteen years. The first sentence is rather pompous. But she soon settles down and speaks without hesitation, breathing carefully, pacing herself, and stressing the points that matter most.

'In wishing you all Good Evening, I feel that I am speaking to friends and companions who have shared with my sister and myself many a happy *Children's Hour*. Thousands of you in this country have had to leave your homes and be separated from your fathers and mothers. My sister Margaret Rose and I feel so much for you, as we know from experience what it means to be away from those we love most of all. . . . We know, every one of us, that in the end all will be well.

On 13th October 1940, Princess Elizabeth, aged fourteen, made her first broadcast, with Princess Margaret at her side. It was the BBC's Children's Hour, listened to by millions of children throughout Britain and the Empire.

For God will care for us, and give us victory and peace. And when peace comes, remember, it will be for *us*, the children of today, to make the world of tomorrow a better and happier place. My sister is by my side and we are both going to say good night to you. Come on Margaret. Good night and good luck to you all.'

The Queen had rehearsed Elizabeth in the techniques of breathing, learnt from Mr Logue. As Elizabeth spoke, she sat beside her and beat out the time. Queen Mary, listening to the wireless at Badminton, noted in her diary with huge satisfaction, 'Excellent ... so natural and unaffected.' Just what was needed in a future Queen. It is not hard to imagine what the King, the proudest of fathers, felt as he listened. He who found public speaking and broadcasting such a burden. The content, with its dogged determination to win through, and its looking ahead to a better future for all, clearly bears his mark. The King, who listened to *Lift Up Your Hearts* every morning on the BBC, wanted his daughter to know that they were fighting for a better and a fairer world. As for Elizabeth herself, she must have felt pleased with a job well done. Then it was back to Windsor. Back to the humdrum daily round.

Weekends were the highpoint of the week. The King and Queen always tried to be back at Windsor by Friday afternoon, in time for a family tea. They needed this semblance of normality as much as their children did. Mid-afternoon on Fridays usually found Marion Crawford and the two princesses, with a couple of corgis and perhaps a pony, wandering along the road on the look-out for the Royal car. 'There was great excitement when the two cars appeared in the distance, the leading one with the King and Queen and Mr Cameron, the King's detective, beside the chauffeur; the second with the equerry and lady-in-waiting,' remembered Marion Crawford in her book *The Little Princesses*. 'We all started to run towards them – horses, dogs and ourselves – and the car slowed down to a crawl and stopped. I remember how tired the King and Queen looked, and how very happy and relieved they were to see their daughters so cheerful and leading a comparatively natural life in spite of the war.'

But by Sunday evening, or at the latest Monday morning, it was back to London. More and more the King and Queen were developing their own style for the role of monarchy during these times of war. They wanted to be, and to be seen to be, at one with their people. The style they developed to go with this was much less formal than before. They walked among the ruins, examining the

Mother and her two daughters in the garden at Windsor in July 1941. A peaceful retreat for the Queen who spent most of the week in war-torn London with her husband.

TOP: An idyllic picture of mother and two daughters on a summer's day, a far cry from the harsh realities of war. ABOVE: The same day, the princesses in the gardens at Windsor, doing their lessons, watched by their mother. RIGHT: Princess Elizabeth at Windsor, safe from the bombs.

damage along with the people who lived and worked there. They talked to them as one person to another, one parent to another, one fighter to another. They felt with the people and the people felt with them. 'This war has drawn the Throne and the people more closely together than was ever before recorded,' Churchill wrote to the King.

George VI's speeches also became increasingly personal in style. 'In this grave hour, perhaps the most fateful in our history, I send every household of my peoples, both at home and overseas, this message, spoken with the same depth of feeling for each one of you as if I were able to cross your threshold and speak to you myself,' he said at the outbreak of war. In 1940, as things got worse, he said, 'The decisive struggle is now upon us. I am going to speak plainly to you, for in this hour of trial I know that you would not have me do otherwise.'

Churchill, in the meantime, was making his famous, rousing speeches. 'We shall fight on the beaches, we shall fight on the landing grounds, we shall fight in the fields and in the streets, we shall fight in the hills; we shall never surrender.' Between them, the King and the Prime Minister made a good team. The other teamwork George VI and Queen Elizabeth fostered was the relationship with America, and with President Roosevelt in particular. American aid and ultimate military involvement was vital to the outcome of the war. The King and Queen had met Roosevelt when they were on their tour of Canada and America in the Spring of 1939. They got on immediately, and had kept up a correspondence ever since. By May 1941, Roosevelt was beginning to persuade the American people of the need for intervention: 'The delivery of needed supplies to Britain is imperative. This can be done. It must be done. It will be done . . .' ending with the famous and powerful truth '. . . the only thing we have to fear is fear itself.'

The King immediately sent a telegram to Roosevelt. 'The Queen and I are deeply grateful for your magnificent speech. It has given us great encouragement and will I know stimulate us all to still greater efforts till the victory for freedom is finally won.'

Wheeler-Bennett, in his biography of George VI, describes a note the King had scribbled to himself, and kept on his desk: 'The schoolboy's definition of courage: That part of you which says "stick it" while the rest of you says "chuck it".' And beneath it he had scribbled a verse from Isaiah: 'They helped every one his neighbour and every one said to his brother, Be of good courage.'

On 1st March 1942, Princess Elizabeth was confirmed. It was the occasion of a rare family reunion at Windsor. Queen Mary came with her old friend Lady Airlie. 'Lilibet much grown, very pretty eyes and complexion, pretty figure.

Princess Elizabeth was gradually being trained to, one day, become Queen. On her sixteenth birthday, she became Colonel of the Grenadier Guards and walked solemnly at her father's side, learning the job.

Margaret very short, intelligent face, but not really pretty,' Queen Mary later wrote to her daughter-in-law Princess Alice. In her diary she wrote, 'Lilibet looked so nice in white with a small veil & was quite composed.' The grandmother could once again feel satisfaction at her grandchild's progress. And it is quite clear which grandchild interested her most.

Another landmark in that progress came a month later, at Elizabeth's sixteenth birthday. She was created Colonel of the Grenadier Guards. In uniform, and walking solemnly at her father's side, she went up and down the lines, inspecting the men, learning the job. She also went to register at the local Labour Exchange for the wartime youth service scheme and from that day a quiet battle went on between father and daughter, as to when she could start some wartime work. As far as the King was concerned, she was far too young. As far as Elizabeth was concerned, she was more than ready.

ABOVE: *The King and Queen liked the family to spend quiet evenings reading, playing cards, knitting and sewing. The King was excellent at needlepoint.*

RIGHT: *George VI and his family in 1942 at one of the rare occasions when the two princesses came up to London during the war.*

In October 1942, Mrs Roosevelt came to see for herself how things were in London. 'Buckingham Palace is an enormous place, and without heat,' she noted in her diary. 'Many of the windows had no glass. The food was war-time food, but it was eaten off gold and silver plate.' Mrs Roosevelt noticed how tense the King seemed throughout dinner. These were critical times: Rommel was being defeated in North Africa, and the Russians were pressing on with their summer offensive. The King's brother, the Duke of Kent, had been killed two months earlier, leaving a widow and their three young children.

After dinner they had a film show. Appropriately it was Noël Coward in a stirring tale of Second World War courage – *In Which We Serve*. At the end, the King finally got up to telephone Downing Street for the latest war news. He came back into the room singing *Roll Out The Barrel*. Good news, evidently.

ABOVE: *Princess Elizabeth, aged sixteen and Princess Margaret aged twelve sitting together reading a book, and still dressed alike.*

RIGHT: *Elizabeth, aged sixteen. This was the year she started her first public engagements.*

Meanwhile, at Badminton, Queen Mary was running out of ivy so she duly replaced her Ivy Squad with her Wooding Squad. Same people, same place, different tidying task. Keen not to use up precious petrol, her preferred method of transport was a farm cart, with two basket chairs in the back for herself and her lady-in-waiting. Off they went to far corners of the estate to clear up the woods. There was also a Salvage Squad in response to a general request from the Ministry of Supply. 'Some of the children (evacuees from Birmingham) came to help,' she noted in her diary, '& we salvaged old bones, tins etc., evidently an old rubbish heap – while others cut down elders – I raked away a lot of rubbish.' When they stopped for a break, Queen Mary liked to have a chat and a cigarette. There were times when her zeal for salvaging, combined with her total lack of knowledge about country life, led her to remove various farm implements left there intentionally by the farmer for later use. These were discreetly returned.

At Windsor, the two princesses were growing up and Marion Crawford saw to it that life wasn't too boring. There was the madrigal group, the parties for Eton boys, the visits from various cousins. They also did a bit of entertaining – mostly lunch parties with members of the household and some officers of the Grenadier Guards or American servicemen. 'Lilibet played the part of hostess perfectly,' writes Miss Crawford in her book. 'She never left anyone hanging around. She chose who would sit on her right and who on her left . . . Lilibet had very natural good manners and was an excellent conversationalist.' In view of all the entertaining Princess Elizabeth was to have to do for the rest of her life, this too was presumably seen as part of the training.

LEFT: Princess Elizabeth and Princess Margaret growing up in the relative security and safety of Windsor during the war.

BELOW: On her sixteenth birthday Princess Elizabeth started to spend more time with her father, learning about his job and preparing for her future role as Queen.

Then there were the pantomimes. Marion Crawford was nothing if not enterprising. She decided that life should be fun, in spite of the war, particularly at Christmas. She suggested a Christmas show and Windsor Castle was, after all, the ideal place for it. There was a good stage in St George's Hall, plenty of props, and heaps of dressing up material. The King and Queen, their minds occupied with more serious matters, gave their consent. They may also have felt it important for Elizabeth to have some fun as she was inclined to be a little too conscientious.

That first Christmas they did a play called *The Christmas Child*. Elizabeth was one of the three kings and wore a velvet tunic and a gold crown. The other two kings were evacuees from London. Margaret, who was a natural actress, played Mary. She sang a solo in front of a hall-full of people. The King and Queen were amazed at the standard of the performance. 'I cried all the way through,' wrote the King.

There followed *Cinderella, Sleeping Beauty, Aladdin* and *Old Mother Red Riding Boots* (a made-up pantomine title), each more ambitious than the last as now Marion Crawford enlisted the help of a local schoolmaster, Hubert Tanner. He had been an actor, and he knew a thing or two about script writing and stage-craft. Miss Betty Vacani, the princesses' ballet teacher, was also roped in. These

The princesses in May 1944 at Windsor. The age gap between Elizabeth, eighteen and Margaret, fourteen seems wider at this stage.

LEFT: *Princess Elizabeth in the Christmas pantomime* Old Mother Red Riding Boots *in 1944.*
RIGHT: *Marion Crawford saw to it that there was also some fun during the war. Every Christmas they put on a pantomime at Windsor Castle. The first was* Cinderella, *with Princess Margaret as Cinderella and Princess Elizabeth as Prince Charming.*

days the King and Queen took a more active part as well, watching the dress rehearsal, and offering suggestions. 'I can't hear a word any of them say,' the King would call from the back of the hall. 'Lilibet cannot possibly wear that,' he said on another occasion. 'The tunic is too short.'

The cast was made up of Mr Tanner's pupils. Usually, Princess Elizabeth played the leading man, and Princess Margaret inevitably took the part of the leading lady. Margaret would always feel sick on the morning of the show, but perform brilliantly in the event. Elizabeth would keep very calm, never showing her feelings, though she was just as excited underneath. The photographs of these pantomimes, taken through the years, are a charming record of two teenage girls growing up. By the time they pose in a cheerful group photograph for *Old Mother Red Riding Boots*, Elizabeth is eighteen. She wears a long, white lace dress and a hat. Her hands are folded in her lap. She looks composed and happy. She has grown up.

Elizabeth's eighteenth birthday was another landmark. Now she was given her own sitting room and a lady-in-waiting. She became a Counsellor of State 'in order that she should have every opportunity of gaining experience in the duties which would fall upon her in the event of her acceding to the Throne.' She was made President of the National Society for the Prevention of Cruelty to Children and on 31st May Elizabeth made her first public speech on their behalf at the Mansion House in London. She must have been nervous and the speech was pompously written, but she carried it off well. The Princess attended her first official banquet, held for the Prime Ministers of the Dominions. She had Field-Marshal Smuts of South Africa on one side, and Mr Mackenzie King of Canada on the other. Mr Mackenzie King thought she was 'not in the least shy and looked very pretty and very happy and graceful'.

'Lilibet's 18th birthday,' wrote the King in his diary at Windsor. 'The Changing of the Guard took place in the quadrangle and we made it an occasion for her birthday . . . We gave a family lunch to which Mama came. It was a lovely hot day. L. can now act as Counsellor of State.'

LEFT: *Princess Elizabeth in 1944 aged eighteen, making her first public speech at the Mansion House.*

BELOW: *When Princess Elizabeth was eighteen she was given her own lady-in-waiting and her own sitting room. This photograph of her at her desk was taken in 1946.*

Pathé News were allowed to make a special feature to mark the birthday. She walks towards the camera on the terrace of Windsor Castle, stops where she has been told to stop, and gazes into the distance. She is clearly not fazed by the cameras which had always been a part of her life.

But it was almost another year before the King would finally let his daughter join the Forces. In April 1945, Princess Elizabeth, aged eighteen, height 5'3", eyes blue, hair brown, became No. 230873 Second Subaltern Elizabeth Alexandra Mary Windsor of the Auxiliary Transport Service at Camberley Mechanical Transport Training Centre. She wore khaki uniform and she learnt all about sparking plugs and car maintenance, map reading and driving in convoy. A course,

LEFT: Princess Elizabeth, aged nearly nineteen, in her ATS uniform, proud to be part of the war effort at last. BELOW: In April 1945 Elizabeth became No. 230873 Second Subaltern of the ATS and eagerly went for training at Camberley Training Centre.

then, entirely to her liking. When her parents came to visit at the end of the course they found her under a car, covered in grease and beaming.

★   ★   ★

On 8th May it was VE Day. Again and again, the King, the Queen, Princess Elizabeth and Princess Margaret came out onto the balcony of Buckingham Palace, waving and smiling and waving again. Below them, as far as the eye could see, was an ocean of people, smiling, laughing and singing, in triumph and in gratitude.

For the two princesses, now nineteen and fifteen, it was unbearable to look down on the jubilant crowd and not be part of them. They begged and pleaded with their parents to let them go until, reluctantly, their parents agreed. So down they went, Elizabeth in her ATS uniform with her cap pulled well down so that no one would recognise her. They went with a small group of friends and their mother's younger brother, Uncle David. They linked arms with the crowd, singing and laughing, and made their way up Whitehall. Uncle David encouraged them to behave as badly as possible. His party piece was to knock a policeman's helmet off from the back, and then catch it at the front. They came back across Green Park and stood outside Buckingham Palace, shouting for the King and Queen along with everyone else. 'We want the King! We want the Queen!' Eventually, they had to send a note up to say that they were waiting outside. Soon enough, out came the King and Queen again, waving and smiling, knowing that somewhere down there among the sea of faces were their two exhilarated daughters.

Queen Mary celebrated VE Day at Badminton. She listened to the King's broadcast on the wireless, and Churchill, and the cheering crowds outside Buckingham Palace. Then she went off down to the pub to celebrate with the local villagers. 'We sang songs, a friendly affair and amusing,' she noted that evening in her diary.

RIGHT TOP: VE Day, 8th May 1995. The Queen Mother with the Queen and Princess Margaret at Buckingham Palace, smiling and waving to the cheering crowds below. RIGHT BELOW: Fifty years earlier, VE Day 8th May 1945. The Royal Family and Winston Churchill on the same famous balcony.

CHAPTER SIX

SOME DAY MY PRINCE WILL COME

ABOVE: Stag night at the Dorchester Hotel. There were twelve guests, every one in Royal Naval evening dress. Philip's uncle, Lord Mountbatten sits to his left, looking highly pleased.

LEFT: 20th November 1947. The Wedding Day. The couple had waited so long to announce their engagement that the wedding came soon after. There were 2 500 wedding presents.

'Poor darlings, they have never had any fun yet,' the King wrote in his diary about his daughters on the evening of VE Day. Which just goes to prove how little parents know of the secret lives of their children. For although life at Windsor during the war was mostly routine and boring, there was something going on in Princess Elizabeth's life which could make even the most boring day hum with hidden excitement.

Elizabeth was in love – the Princess had a Prince. She saw very little of him because he was away at war, but every now and again a letter would arrive from him and the day would be transformed. First love is a magical thing, but no one expects it to last. The extraordinary thing about Princess Elizabeth's first love is that it did last, from the day, aged thirteen, that she first met him, to the day they married. Since then, there have been ups and downs, as in all marriages, but today they are still together, still a good team.

John Wheeler-Bennett, in his definitive biography of George VI, is once again the witness. 'This was the man with whom Princess Elizabeth had been in love from their first meeting. A cousinly correspondence was maintained throughout the war and Prince Philip spent several of his rare leaves at Windsor, where on at least one occasion he entertained King George with an account of his adventures in the Mediterranean.' Wheeler-Bennett's biography was published in 1958, with Royal approval. The Queen and Prince Philip will therefore have read it before publication. They didn't correct the story nor did they insist that it be taken out.

There is, as it happens, a photograph which marks the occasion of that first meeting between Prince and Princess. It was taken on 22nd July 1939, and the occasion was the Royal Family's visit to the Royal Naval College at Dartmouth. It is a riveting photograph, capturing as it does a split moment in time, with all the main players in the unfolding drama there for everyone to see.

The King had brought his family up the River Dart in the Royal Yacht *Victoria and Albert* for a short cruise in the summer of 1939, following his and the Queen's return from their pre-war visit to America. The family of four was together again, and the King wanted to show them Dartmouth, the Royal Naval College where he had been a cadet. They were accompanied by Lord Louis Mountbatten, who had himself been a cadet at Dartmouth. Mountbatten was a cousin of the King's (and coincidentally Uncle to Prince Philip), and a friend. In fact he had been one of Edward VIII's greatest friends, and after the Abdication he turned his attentions to George VI, giving him support when he needed it most. Many said that Mountbatten was always looking out for the main chance, but be that as it may, both George VI and the Queen counted him amongst their best friends.

On 22nd July 1939 the Royal family visited the Royal Naval College at Dartmouth. It was the first time Elizabeth (on the left), aged thirteen, and Philip (on the right at the back, in uniform) met.

The photograph was taken as the Royal family watched a gym display by the cadets. They are up in a gallery looking down on the gym. The King is watching the display. He looks as though his thoughts are caught up in past memories. The Queen is turning to listen to a naval officer who is probably explaining what's going on. Princess Margaret, beside her mother and now nine years old, is watching the display, looking a bit bored. Princess Elizabeth, as ever dressed identically to her younger sister, is further along, also watching the display. She has her usual contained, serious expression. Behind them stands a group of three men who are in quite a different mood from the Royal family. They are highly animated, and absolutely not watching the display. There is a roguish-looking man in a suit, laughing. There is Mountbatten, looking straight at the camera, debonair, charming and knowing. And beside him, very animated and telling some anecdote, stands Philip, Mountbatten's nephew. Philip was just eighteen, and a cadet at Dartmouth, but he was not part of the gym display because he had been deputed, by his uncle, to look after the two princesses.

There is also an account of what happened next. Marion Crawford was present on the visit to Dartmouth. She is probably the half-hidden person sitting next to Princess Elizabeth in the photograph. She described the visit in some detail in her book – her account may be a little romanticised, but she won't have made it up entirely.

As it happens, some of the cadets had developed mumps, so the two princesses spent a lot of their time at the Captain's house, playing in the nursery and Marion Crawford went with them. 'After a time a fair-haired boy, rather like a Viking, with a sharp face and piercing blue eyes, came in. He was good-looking, though rather off-hand in his manner.' That was Philip. He was soon bored with playing in the nursery and suggested they go off to the tennis courts. Not to play tennis, but to jump the nets – have some fun. For two very protected princesses, you can see the attraction. He led, they followed.

'How good he is, Crawfie. How high he can jump,' Marion Crawford remembers Princess Elizabeth saying. Miss Crawford, being a bit prim at times, thought him a bit of a show-off. 'She never took her eyes off him the whole time,' she adds. 'He was polite to her, but did not pay her any special attention. He spent a lot of time teasing plump little Margaret.'

Apparently, Philip went on board the Royal Yacht for lunch, and there was a lot of talk and laughter. He went on board again for dinner, but Elizabeth wasn't there. She had gone to bed.

When the Royal Yacht left Dartmouth, the cadets were allowed to get into any small boat available and follow the *Victoria and Albert* down river, giving her a royal send-off. After a while they stopped trying to keep up and turned back. All but one cadet, rowing for all he was worth. The King and Mountbatten finally had to shout at him through a megaphone before Philip would give up and turn back.

So who was this Philip? The answer often given is that he was a penniless Prince with no Kingdom, and a schoolboy with no proper home. This is accurate enough, but it somehow falls short of the truth. Prince Philip of Greece was born on the island of Corfu on 10th June 1921. His father, Prince Andrew of Greece, was away fighting the Turks. Prince Andrew was the son of the King of Greece, but he was not Greek. His father was Danish, his mother was Russian. (With Royal families, everyone seems to come from somewhere else.) So when Marion Crawford described Philip as a Viking, she wasn't far off the mark.

Philip's mother was Princess Alice of Battenberg and her family had come over from Germany to England and changed their name to Mountbatten. Louis Mountbatten was her younger brother. Alice was born virtually deaf. Philip was her fifth and last child, and her only son. One could imagine this creating a strong bond between mother and child. Douglas Keay notes in his book *Elizabeth II, Portrait of a Monarch* that before Philip was born, his mother wrote to her brother Louis in England, 'If the child will be a boy, he will be sixth in succession to the Greek throne.' The thought was already there.

Philip was barely one when revolutionary troubles started up again in Greece. The family had to go into exile in a hurry, and it was George V – Princess Elizabeth's beloved grandfather – who sent a ship to get them out. Prince Andrew was a cousin, and Princess Alice was Louis Mountbatten's sister. On both counts, George V wasn't going to leave them to their fate. The family ended up in St Cloud outside Paris, in a largish villa, but with no money to speak of. Exile put more strain on a marriage which was anyway based on two people of extreme opposites. Philip's mother, perhaps because of her deafness, was quiet and withdrawn. Later in life she founded an order of nuns, the order of Mary and Martha. She wore a grey habit and led a reclusive life. She died at Buckingham Palace in 1969. But Philip's father was an extrovert, active man. When exile deprived him

Prince Philip's parents, Prince Andrew and Princess Alice of Greece, had little in common and by the time Philip was ten they were living apart.

of his military career, he spent most of his time in Paris cafés with other exiles, talking obsessively about getting back to Greece. He died in Monte Carlo in 1944. So the parents were complete opposites and gradually they drifted apart.

Philip's first eight years were spent at St Cloud. It was a female-dominated household, and he may have been a bit spoilt. He was certainly extremely high spirited and did pretty much as he pleased. The family spoke English at home, but also some Greek and French and German. So it was a cosmopolitan childhood, very unlike Princess Elizabeth's, spent within the narrow confines of British royal family life.

When he was eight, Philip came to England, to Cheam Preparatory School. His Mountbatten cousin, David, was already there. 'Very charming and mischievous,' a teacher recalled of Philip when talking to Tim Heald for his biography *The Duke*. He was bright, but not particularly academic, and, right from the start, a great athlete. He won at high jump (as we know from the tennis court incident), diving, and hurdles. He was full of energy and fun. From Cheam, Philip often went home with David for weekends and holidays. So his mother's side of the family, the Mountbattens, became very important in his life.

After Cheam, Philip did a short stint at Salem in Germany. (All four of his sisters had married into the German aristocracy.) His parents' marriage had finally broken down and the house at St Cloud was gone. So, aged ten, Philip was left effectively homeless and Germany probably seemed the natural place for him to go. But the Nazis were by now in power, and that didn't go down too well. Philip came back to Britain, back into the sphere of the Mountbatten family and the English way of doing things. From Greece to France to England to Germany and back to England again.

He went to school at Gordonstoun in Scotland. Gordonstoun had just been started up by a German Jew who had fled Nazi Germany where he had been arrested for his outspoken criticism of the Nazis. Dr Kurt Hahn was one of life's extraordinary men. Unconventional, charismatic, and progressive, 'I do not like schoolmasters', he once said – an unusual thing for a schoolmaster to say perhaps.

LEFT ABOVE: *Philip was the youngest of five children and the only boy. He was lively and mischievous from the start, and perhaps a little spoilt.*

LEFT BELOW: *Philip, (2nd from the left) aged seven. By now the family was living in exile at St Cloud outside Paris. Soon he was to come to England, to Cheam Preparatory School, and into the care of the Mountbattens, his grandparents on his mother's side.*

But one gets the point: he didn't want conventional men teaching his boys. Dr Hahn was completely un-English in his approach, and Gordonstoun was quite unlike any other conventional English public school of the time. Hahn, more than anyone, influenced the young and, like himself, displaced Philip.

Gordonstoun was a small school to start with, and Philip was soon the star. Hahn later said of Philip that he was 'often naughty, never nasty'. In his final report he tellingly summed him up. 'He is universally trusted, liked and respected. He has the greatest sense of service of all the boys in the school. Philip is a born leader, but will need the exacting demands of a great service to do justice to himself. His best is outstanding – his second best is not good enough.' Who knows where the sense of service came from, but it was certainly to come in useful in later life. By the time the report was written, Philip, influenced no doubt by his uncle Louis Mountbatten, had opted for a career in the Royal Navy, and was on his way to Dartmouth.

This, then, was the Philip Princess Elizabeth met on that day in July 1939. Connected to all the Royal families in Europe, strikingly good-looking and charming, full of energy and optimism, and yet an outsider, pretty much penniless, and, when all is said and done, homeless. To him the Royal family must have looked enviably stable and loving. To her, he must have promised all the thrill and adventure which her own family lacked.

Gossip spreads fast, and it wasn't long before there was quite a bit of it going round what was in those days referred to as 'society'. Freda Dudley Ward, Edward VIII's one-time mistress, was full of it. So was Chips Channon, a rich and well-connected American who had married Lady Honor Guinness and settled in England. He published his diaries in 1967 and they have been quoted ever since. As early as January 1941, he was writing, on return from a cocktail party also attended by Prince Philip, 'He is extraordinarily handsome ... he is to be our Prince Consort, and that is why he is serving in our Royal Navy.'

The whole of London 'society' was talking about the romance and they went on talking about it for the next five years. Officially it was constantly denied. At Windsor, though, there was a special guest at the 1943 Christmas pantomime, *Aladdin*. Princess Elizabeth was seventeen, and looked very different from the thirteen-year-old little girl Philip had played with at Dartmouth. Philip, looking more handsome than ever in his naval uniform, was rolling about, laughing at the awful jokes. 'I have never known Lilibet more animated,' wrote Marion Crawford.

At Gordonstoun his headmaster, Kurt Hahn, wrote of Philip: 'His best is outstanding – his second best is not good enough.'

'There was a sparkle about her none of us had ever seen before. Many people remarked on it.'

On 17th March 1944, George VI wrote to his mother at Badminton: 'We both think she is too young for that now, as she has never met any young men of her own age.' The King and Queen were so taken up with war work that they were apparently unaware of the entertaining, mostly arranged by Miss Crawford, that went on at Windsor. He went on: 'I like Philip. He is intelligent, has a good sense of humour & thinks about things in the right way ... We are going to tell George [of Greece] that P. had better not think any more about it for the present.'

This was written, Sir John Wheeler-Bennett, George VI's official biographer, tells us, after George of Greece had broached the matter with the King. But George must have felt encouraged. They liked Philip, but more importantly, they felt he thought about things 'in the right way'. Queen Mary, reading that, would have known exactly what that meant. To marry into the Royal family, as she knew only too well, you had to think of things 'in the right way'.

When Basil Boothroyd was writing his authorised biography of Prince Philip in 1971, Philip had this to say about all the gossip: 'It had been mentioned, presumably, that "he is eligible, he's the sort of person she might marry." I mean, after all, if you spend ten minutes thinking about it – and a lot of these people spent a great deal more time thinking about it – how many obviously eligible young men, other than people living in this country, were available? Inevitably I must have been on the list, so to speak.'

People can negotiate as much as they like, but unless the person themself is willing, they can't get very far. Philip, in the same interview, said this about his own involvement: 'I suppose one thing led to another. I suppose I began to think about it seriously, oh, let me think now, when I got back in '46 and went to Balmoral. It was probably then that we, that it became, you know, that we began to think seriously, and even talk about it.' This is a wonderfully understated answer. It doesn't take much imagination to work out what a difficult decision it must have been for the Prince, regardless of whether he was in love with Princess Elizabeth or not. Though judging by the evidence in the photographs at the time, and the accounts of people close to them, he certainly was. The difficult decision lay in the way of life he would have to accept. The lack of freedom, the call to duty, and always having to take second place to his wife.

Princess Elizabeth and Princess Margaret in Aladdin *the pantomime Philip came to see during the war at Windsor. He found a very different girl from the thirteen-year-old he'd met at Dartmouth.*

Prince Philip in naval uniform and with a beard, the photograph Princess Elizabeth kept on her dressing table during the last year of the war.

Philip had come back from the war, like everyone else who had seen active service, an older and a wiser man. He had had what is called a 'good war', been mentioned in despatches for his part in the Battle of Matapan in 1941, and ended the war as one of the youngest First Lieutenants in the Navy. There had been plenty of girls everywhere Philip went. And he had made some great friends, none more so than the Australian Mike Parker, who later became his equerry. 'He never said anything to me, and I never said anything to him,' Mike Parker told Tim Heald for his book *The Duke*. But when the engagement was finally announced Mike Parker wasn't surprised.

In the first instance, the King and Queen were only prepared to accept a private engagement. Officially the rumours were still denied. The King still felt Princess Elizabeth, now twenty, was too young. Perhaps her adoring and over-protective father wasn't ready to let her go. But Princess Elizabeth's mind was made up, and had been for a long time. She didn't want Hugh Fitzroy, Earl of Euston, nor Charles Manners, Duke of Rutland. Both were eminently suitable in the conventional way: Eton, Cambridge and the Grenadier Guards. But Elizabeth didn't want someone conventional, which sheds an interesting light on the Princess.

However, Philip was so unconventional that he was viewed, and went on being viewed, with deep suspicion by some of the courtiers. For a start, he wasn't a British subject. And he didn't have a surname. He had no money, and no home. His father had died in Monte Carlo, and everyone knew what Monte Carlo was like. His mother was some kind of a nun. And his three sisters (one having been tragically killed in an air crash before the war) were all married to Germans if not Nazis.

As far as the King and Queen were concerned, none of that bothered them. But first things first. And duty always comes first. Princess Elizabeth and Princess Margaret were to accompany their parents on a Royal Tour of South Africa. To thank the South Africans, and General Smuts in particular, for having supported Britain in the war. They set off on HMS *Vanguard* from Portsmouth on 31st January 1947. Queen Mary, now safely ensconced in Marlborough House again, came to see them off. Philip gave Elizabeth a record, as well as the photograph, to remember him by. It was *People will say we're in love*, and they say she drove everyone mad playing it over and over again.

In Britain, it was the worst winter for years. The snow and ice, combined with the terrible shortages of coal and everything else following six years of war, made life hard to bear. Is this the peace we fought for, people were beginning to ask themselves. The King felt he should be staying with his people. The Government felt he should go and do his duty in the warm sunshine of South Africa. From South Africa the King wrote to Queen Mary: 'I am very worried over the extra privations which all of you at home are having to put up with in this ghastly cold weather with no light or fuel. In many ways I wish I was with you having borne so many trials with them.' The Queen kept him steady as always. She, too, wrote to Queen Mary: 'The tour is being very strenuous as I feared it would be & doubly hard for Bertie who feels he should be at home. But there is very little he could do now, and even if he interrupted his tour & flew home, it would be very exhausting...'

Princess Elizabeth celebrated her twenty-first birthday out in South Africa. To mark the occasion, she made a filmed broadcast to the whole of the Commonwealth from Government House in Cape Town. Seen now, it is a very touching broadcast in which this young woman dedicates herself to a life of service. 'I should like to make that dedication now,' she said, looking straight at the camera and speaking slowly and clearly as she had done when rehearsing the speech with her father. She looks young and beautiful. Too young, almost, for the heavy burden

RIGHT ABOVE: 1995. South Africa's President, Nelson Mandela and Queen Elizabeth walk to the parliament building from his office in Cape Town. The start of the Queen's first visit to the country since 1947.

RIGHT BELOW: On her twenty-first birthday, Princess Elizabeth made her speech of dedication from Cape Town. 'I declare before you all that my whole life, whether it be long or short, shall be devoted to your service . . .'

BELOW: Princess Elizabeth and Princess Margaret in South Africa early in 1947. King George VI and Queen Elizabeth wanted Princess Elizabeth to put Philip out of her mind and enjoy the tour. They felt she was too young to be thinking about an engagement.

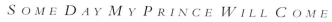

of the words that follow. 'It is very simple. I declare before you all that my whole life, whether it be long or short, shall be devoted to your service and the service of our great Imperial Commonwealth to which we all belong. But I shall not have strength to carry out this resolution unless you join in it with me, as I now invite you to do; I know that your support will be unfailingly given. God bless all of you who are willing to share it.'

She did not hesitate or waver. Queen Mary, listening to the broadcast at Marlborough House, must have nodded approvingly. That was what she had done, and that is what Elizabeth would do. Prince Philip must have felt proud but another part must have quaked at what it meant.

Three days later the Royal family were on their way home. Whilst they were away Philip's naturalisation papers came through, so he was now a British subject. The final obstacle to the announcement of the engagement was removed.

The family arrived back on 12th May 1947 and Queen Mary was at Buckingham Palace to greet them – along with a tumultuous crowd. So, no doubt, was Philip. But the King held out for another two months. He couldn't bear to let her go. And there was the small matter of Philip's surname. The King and the Prime Minister thought His Royal Highness Prince Philip would do. Philip thought otherwise. He wanted a plain surname. They settled for the name on his mother's side of the family – Mountbatten. His uncle, Lord Louis Mountbatten, the great campaigner, must have seen it as a victory.

On 10th July 1947, a notice was pinned to the railings at Buckingham Palace: 'It is with the greatest of pleasure that the King and Queen announce the betrothal of their dearly beloved daughter, The Princess Elizabeth, to Lieutenant Philip Mountbatten, R.N., son of the late Prince Andrew of Greece and Princess Andrew (Alice of Battenberg), to which union the King has gladly given his consent'.

The photographs and the Pathé newsreel of the couple on the day of their engagement shine out with the happiness of the future bride and her handsome Prince. Queen Mary wrote in her diary: 'Heard with great pleasure of darling Lilibet's engagement to Philip Mountbatten. They both came to see me after luncheon looking radiant.' She gave Lilibet a present of the jewellery which had been her own wedding present in 1893. Later that month the couple appeared together at a Buckingham Palace garden party. They did indeed look radiant, she in a summer dress and hat, he in his rather worn naval uniform. Princess Elizabeth displayed her diamond engagement ring, just like any other bride-to-be.

Princess Elizabeth's twenty-first birthday pictures were taken in South Africa – a long way from the bleak English winter, and from Philip to whom she was secretly, informally engaged.

ABOVE: *On 10th July a notice was pinned to the railings at Buckingham Palace: 'It is with the greatest of pleasure that the King and Queen announce the betrothal of their dearly beloved daughter, the Princess Elizabeth, to Lieutenant Philip Mountbatten, RN . . .'*

LEFT: *At the garden party at Buckingham Palace Princess Elizabeth and Prince Philip, newly engaged, walked amongst the guests looking very happy and showing off the engagement ring.*

Having waited so long to get engaged, the couple had no intention of waiting longer still to get married and the wedding was on 20th November 1947. In another winter of austerity it was the occasion of wild enthusiasm. Only the *Daily Worker* and a couple of Trade Unionists complained at the expense. Everyone else saw it as a glorious escape from the daily grind. They were certain it was a love match, *Cinderella* and *The Sleeping Beauty* wrapped into one. The crowds queued up in the cold outside St James's Palace to file past the vast array of wedding presents. There were 2 500 of them, including a fine set of pearls from the bride's parents and a tea cloth which some called a loin cloth from Mr Gandhi, woven by himself.

Two nights before the wedding, there was a party at Buckingham Palace. Queen Mary had a splendid time. 'Saw many old friends,' she wrote. 'I stood from 9.30 till 12.15 a.m.!!! Not bad for 80'. The following evening it was Philip Mountbatten's stag night at the Dorchester Hotel. There were a dozen guests, and every one was in Royal Naval evening dress. There was Philip's cousin David who had been at Cheam Preparatory School with him all those years ago and who was his best man. There was Mike Parker, the friend he made during the war and who was about to become his equerry. And, of course, there was Lord Louis Mountbatten looking, in the official photographs of the occasion, like someone who has just won the Pools.

The next day was the wedding. Part of it was to be televised. It seemed as if the whole world had stopped what it was doing to be there. 'I was so proud of you and thrilled at having you so close to me on our long walk in Westminster Abbey,' the King wrote to his beloved daughter later, 'but when I handed your hand to the Archbishop I felt that I had lost something very precious. You were so calm and composed during the Service & said your words with such conviction, that I knew everything was all right. . . . Our family, us four, the "Royal Family" must remain together with additions of course at suitable moments!! I have watched you grow up all these years with pride under the skilful direction of Mummy, who as you know is the most marvellous person in the World in my eyes, & I can, I know, always count on you, & now Philip, to help us in our work. Your leaving us has left a great blank in our lives but do remember that your old home is still yours & do come back to it as much & as often as possible. I can see that you are sublimely happy with Philip which is right but don't forget us is the wish of Your ever loving and devoted Papa.'

Princess Elizabeth and Lt Philip Mountbatten on their wedding day, 20th November 1947.

CHAPTER SEVEN

CORONATION

ABOVE: A street party in Fulham for the Coronation. Most people were only too glad for a reason to celebrate and to forget the years of austerity which followed the war.

LEFT: The Coronation coach on the way to Westminster Abbey on 2nd June 1953. 'The whole of London is full of stands for the Coronation', wrote Queen Mary. 'Too ugly. And the poor daffodils are squashed and hidden underneath.'

When Princess Elizabeth and Prince Philip married they had no idea that there would be less than five years of carefree life before Princess Elizabeth had to take on the heavy burden of the Crown.

They went off on their honeymoon in the highest of spirits after waving long and happily to the crowds from the usual stage of the Buckingham Palace balcony. They left the Palace in an open carriage, rugs over their knees to protect them against the November cold. Beneath the rugs, unseen by the cheering crowds, they had hot water bottles and Susan, Princess Elizabeth's favourite corgi. Once they'd gone, Marion Crawford recalls, the crowds slowly dispersed, the Palace fell silent, and Princess Margaret and the King and Queen were alone.

The couple went first to Broadlands, Lord Mountbatten's home in Hampshire. Locals remember them driving around in Prince Philip's little sports car, singing at the tops of their voices. After four days they went to Birkhall in Scotland, where Elizabeth had spent so many of her childhood summers.

When they got back to London they had to live, in the first instance, with the parents-in-law. They moved in to a suite of rooms at Buckingham Palace, and Prince Philip went off to work at the Admiralty every morning, often on foot. Usually he got back at about five. Marion Crawford describes how the two princesses would often stand at a window watching out for him as he strode back up the Mall. During the day Princess Margaret, now seventeen, still did her lessons with Miss Crawford. Princess Elizabeth went out to functions and did her mountainous correspondence with her lady-in-waiting. Once Philip got back it was time to have some fun.

Life at the Palace was not easy for Prince Philip. Depending on your point of view, he was either a breath of fresh air in that rather stuffy and formalised atmosphere, or he stuck out like a sore thumb. He liked informality and he wandered round the corridors, usually filled with courtiers wearing suits, in a pair of casual trousers and with his sleeves rolled up. His manner matched the clothes and it very often didn't match the way things were normally done. Princess Elizabeth must have done a certain amount of pacifying.

The King and Queen were a different problem. It lay, essentially, in 'the four of us'. As soon as the couple were back from the honeymoon and moved in to Buckingham Palace the four of them seemed to fall imperceptibly back into place. It wasn't easy to make the four into a five.

RIGHT ABOVE: *Princess Elizabeth and Prince Philip on the first part of their honeymoon at Broadlands.*
RIGHT BELOW: *By the end of 1947 'The four of us' had become 'the five of us'.*

LEFT: The Garter Ceremony in 1947 and (ABOVE) in 1995. When Princess Elizabeth and Prince Philip married, King George VI made them both members of the Order of the Garter.

Barely a year after the wedding their first child was born. A son. Princess Elizabeth insisted on giving birth in her own bedroom, which was where the princesses' nursery had once been. It was not yet fashionable for fathers to be present, and Philip took himself off for a game of squash with his old friend and now equerry, Mike Parker. A noisy crowd waited outside the Palace all day for news. Finally the King's Press Secretary, Commander Richard Colville, came out of the Palace, walked across the forecourt, and pinned a hand-written note on the railings:

'The Princess Elizabeth, Duchess of Edinburgh, was safely delivered of a Prince at 9.14 p.m. Her Royal Highness and her son are both doing well'.

Prince Philip just managed to get to the bedside in time to welcome his son, Charles, into the world with a bottle of champagne. For his wife he had a bunch of flowers. Twelve temporary typists were employed to get through the sackfuls of congratulatory letters. 'I can hardly believe he's mine,' the Princess wrote to her old music teacher.

Charles' christening was on 15th December, in the Music Room at Buckingham Palace. 'I gave the baby a silver cup & cover which George III had given to a godson in 1780,' wrote Queen Mary with some satisfaction in her diary that evening, 'so that I gave a present from my (great) grandfather to my great grandson 168 years later.' This was the kind of continuity Queen Mary approved of and had based her life on. It was the essence of monarchy. From her vantage point that day she could look back into the mists of time and forward into the hazy future, and know that although many things change, some do not.

As Tim Heald points out in his fascinating biography of Prince Philip, *The Duke*, the birth of Prince Charles had a less salutary effect on Philip. It made him more peripheral. 'He was the son-in-law of the King, the husband of the future Queen, the father of the future King. In this sense, therefore, he existed primarily in relation to others.'

At the beginning of 1949 the small family finally moved in to a home of their own, Clarence House (which later became the Queen Mother's London home). It was only just up the road from Buckingham Palace, but it was separate, and they had a separate household staff to go with it. Mike Parker was still the equerry, 'Jock' Colville was the Private Secretary: Jock was Lady Cynthia's son, and Lady

Princess Elizabeth's first child, Prince Charles, was born barely a year after the wedding. There was already an heir to the throne.

Cynthia was Queen Mary's lady-in-waiting, but he was young and he came from the Foreign Office, so he wasn't a regular courtier. Then there was the Comptroller of the Household, Lieutenant-General 'Boy' Browning. Browning was the husband of the writer Daphne Du Maurier, and formerly Mountbatten's chief of staff. He was the only older member of this very young and very lively team. Lastly, but certainly not least, there was Bobo – the indispensible Bobo Mcdonald – to attend Princess Elizabeth, John Dean to attend Prince Philip, and the nurse to attend the baby, Prince Charles.

Prince Philip put his stamp on life at Clarence House from the start. The rooms, all redecorated and modernised, were light and airy. The mood was optimistic. From the moment they moved in, life was energetic and fun.

It made a sad contrast with life at Buckingham Palace where the King was ill again. His left foot had gone numb, then his right. The doctors diagnosed a form of thrombosis and decided to operate. The operation went well, but a slight gloom remained. A previously planned Royal Tour of Australia and New Zealand was postponed. The King was inclined to be pessimistic about the state of the country in this difficult post-war era. The Queen was worried about his health. Princess Margaret meanwhile was rather disorientated, alone without her sister for the first time in her life.

That autumn, Prince Philip got the promotion he had been waiting for. He was appointed First Lieutenant and Second-in-Command of HMS *Chequers* with the Mediterranean Fleet. He was based in Malta, where Princess Elizabeth joined him as much as possible. They lived in the Mountbattens' Villa Guardamangia, and led a life which was closer to normal life than at any other time in their marriage. Princess Elizabeth was, for a short time, a naval wife. She shopped, she went to the hairdresser, she spent time with other naval wives. She still had Bobo and a footman, but it must have felt wonderfully informal to her.

Christmas 1949 was spent in Malta. By the spring, Princess Elizabeth was pregnant again, and she returned to Clarence House. Prince Philip came back in July and the baby was born on 15th August 1950. It was a girl, and she was christened Anne Elizabeth Alice Louise. Anne, for the name George V rejected for Princess Margaret, Elizabeth for the two Elizabeths, mother and grandmother, Alice for the other grandmother, and Louise for the Queen of Sweden who was a shared relation, or just for luck.

Princess Elizabeth and Prince Philip in Malta where the Prince was appointed as First Lieutenant and Second-in-Command of HMS Chequers with the Mediterranean Fleet.

When Prince Philip was posted to Malta, the couple had a more normal married life than they would later be able to enjoy.

That same morning, Prince Philip got his next promotion: Lieutenant-Commander, in command of his own ship – the frigate HMS *Magpie*. On board he was known as 'Dukey'. He was tough, expected extremely high standards of everyone, including himself, and he was popular. In other words, he was still the same Philip who had been Kurt Hahn's star pupil at Gordonstoun. People said he had the makings of a First Sea Lord.

However, life had another role in store for the Prince and, in many ways, a more difficult one. By the Spring of 1951, George VI was ill again. On 31st May the King wrote to his mother: 'At last the doctors have found the cause of the

Princess Elizabeth and Prince Philip – proud parents of Princess Anne who was born on 15th August 1950 and christened Anne Elizabeth Alice Louise after her mother and her two grandmothers.

temperature. I have a condition on the left lung known as pneumonitis. It is not pneumonia though if left it might become it ... Everyone is very relieved at this revelation and the doctors are happier about me tonight than they have been for a week.' In fact, the King had cancer.

Princess Elizabeth took over some of her father's work. On 1st July 1951, Prince Philip took indefinite leave from the Navy. At the time he didn't know it was the end of his naval career, but he probably had a shrewd idea. At the Trooping the Colour that year, the King rode in a carriage and Princess Elizabeth rode on her horse, beside him.

LEFT: *Trooping the Colour, 1951. King George VI was ill so Princess Elizabeth took his place, fitting naturally into the role.*

BELOW: *Elizabeth Trooping the Colour in 1995, the yearly ceremony that marks her official birthday.*

By September, the King's doctors felt they had to operate. The Duke of Windsor, the long lost and exiled brother, the man who should have been King, found some pretext to come over from France on a visit to London. Queen Mary had seen her son once after the war, in October 1945, and they corresponded. But to all intents and purposes, he was a figure of the past and now he waited for news in the house of a friend. The night before the operation, the King instructed the Master of the Household to send the Duke of Windsor three brace of grouse, to remind the two brothers of happy summers spent in Scotland all those years ago. Summers spent on the moors and in the heather, oblivious of all the traumatic events which lay ahead. 'I understand he is fond of grouse', the King added, as though he were talking of someone he hardly knew any more. All day the crowds gathered outside Buckingham Palace for news. When the operation was pronounced a success there was an audible sigh of relief.

By October 1951, the great British public was ready for another General Election. They voted out Attlee, the man who had worked so hard for a better post-war Britain, and they voted in Churchill, the hero of the war and a great statesman, now aged seventy-six. Princess Elizabeth and Prince Philip, continuing in their role of stand-ins for the King and Queen, went on a tour of Canada and the USA. As the King and Queen had done before them, the couple left their children behind. On the tour they were mobbed wherever they went: she was a lovely Princess, he a handsome Prince. They were young and full of life – a fairytale come true. The tour was a huge success and on their return the King made them both Privy Councillors, as a token of his gratitude. He felt well again, and looked forward to many years of training his daughter for her future role as Queen and Head of Commonwealth. For Queen Elizabeth it must have been heart-rending to watch. She knew he hadn't long to live.

That Christmas, the King had to prerecord his broadcast because of his bad chest and hoarse voice. For the man who had suffered so many agonies in the past about broadcasting and public speaking, it must have felt like sweet relief. '. . . by the grace of God and through the faithful skill of my doctors, surgeons and nurses I have come through my illness, but I have learned once again that it is in bad times that we value most highly the support and sympathy of our friends.' He read out the sentences in short bursts. 'This support and sympathy has reached me, and I thank you now from my heart . . .'

A photograph which the Queen keeps on her desk. A last picture of grandfather and grandson, on Prince Charles's third birthday.

Another 'Family of Four'. In 1951 the Edinburgh family was still living at Clarence House and Prince Philip was still the head of the family.

On 30th January 1952 the Royal family, the five of them, went to see the hit musical *South Pacific* at Drury Lane Theatre. They were celebrating the King's recovery and giving Princess Elizabeth and Prince Philip a happy send-off, for the following day the couple were leaving on their tour of East Africa, Australia and New Zealand. The children were to be left at Sandringham, with their grandparents and Princess Margaret.

Elizabeth and Philip went to say goodbye to Queen Mary at Marlborough House. 'I felt very sad at having to take leave for such a long time,' Queen Mary wrote. The next day she listened to the farewell scenes at London Airport on the wireless. The King, looking ill and drawn, stood on the tarmac and waved goodbye to his beloved daughter, not knowing that this was his final goodbye.

The tour was meant to last over five months. It lasted just six days. On 5th February, the King went out shooting at Sandringham. He was in good spirits and seemed in better health. That evening Princess Margaret played for him on the piano. The King went to bed at about 10.30. He died in his sleep. He was just 56.

Elizabeth and Philip had by then reached Treetops Hotel in Kenya. Lieutenant-Commander Michael Parker, the equerry, and Lady Pamela Mountbatten, the lady-in-waiting and the Princess's cousin, were with them. They spent the night at the hotel, a glorified tree house, watching the elephants, baboons and rhinos who came to drink at the watering-hole below. Princess Elizabeth, dressed in slacks, spent most of the night filming them on her cine-camera. The next morning they returned to Sagana Hunting Lodge where the rest of the retinue, including Bobo and John Dean, were staying.

Treetops in Kenya, the glorified tree house where Princess Elizabeth and Prince Philip spent the night watching the wildlife, as news came through of the death of her father, George VI.

News travelled slowly in those days. At lunchtime, Martin Charteris, now Princess Elizabeth's Assistant Private Secretary, was told by one of the press that a Reuter's wire had just come through saying the King had died. It took some time to confirm the shocking news. Charteris then told Michael Parker who, in turn, told Prince Philip. Philip walked Princess Elizabeth round the gardens of Sagana Lodge, and they walked and they talked for a long time. Everyone else kept their distance and held their breath.

As they walked around the garden, Princess Elizabeth and Prince Philip tried to take in what had happened, and what their life would be from now on. She was twenty-five, he was thirty. Princess Elizabeth had lost a loving and devoted father, who had protected her all her life. Now he was dead and the protection was gone. She was the Queen and her life was changed for ever. Philip's loss was less personal. But his naval career was at an end, and so, in many senses, was his freedom.

Those who were there, Martin Charteris, Lady Pamela Mountbatten, Michael Parker, were struck and moved by the way Elizabeth took the news. Inwardly she was shocked and grief-stricken. But her own temperament and years of training meant that, outwardly at least, she was calm and composed. She set to work immediately. Whilst others started packing for the long journey home, the Queen sat at the desk writing letters and telegrams to her family, and apologies to those awaiting her in Australia and New Zealand. When Martin Charteris asked her, hesitantly, what she wished to be called as Queen, she looked up in surprise. 'My own name, of course – what else?' And with that she signed 'Elizabeth R' for the first time.

It was Prince Philip who showed the shock. Michael Parker remembers him slumped in an armchair with a newspaper spread over his face. 'I never felt so sorry for anyone in all my life,' he said. 'He looked as if you'd dropped half the world on him.'

It took fifteen hours to fly back to London Airport. On the tarmac waited Churchill, Eden, Attlee and the Duke of Gloucester, her uncle. All were dressed in black. Inside the BOAC plane Queen Elizabeth, as she now was, had also put on her black mourning. 'Shall I go down alone?' she wondered. Philip, accepting his position from now on, stepped back.

The newsreel footage of that moment, taken from the tarmac, has acquired a timeless quality. The plane door swings open and a small figure in black steps out, hesitates for a moment, and then goes slowly and carefully down the steps. Quite alone. A minute later her husband, Prince Philip, follows.

The couple got back to Clarence House at four. Hushed crowds stood outside. Half an hour later Queen Mary arrived in her black limousine from Marlborough

House. 'Her old Grannie and subject must be the first to kiss Her hand,' she said.

The next morning the young Queen Elizabeth walked from Clarence House to St James's Palace next door, for her first meeting with her Privy Counsellors. She read her Declaration of Sovereignty to a room of men all in deep mourning and all at least twice her age. Except, of course, for Philip, her husband. 'My heart is too full,' she said, 'for me to say more to you today than that I shall always work as my father did.' As soon as possible Philip led her away, back to Clarence House. From there they went up to Sandringham to join their children, Princess Margaret and the Queen, now the Queen Mother.

It is hard to imagine how the Queen Mother must have felt. She had known the King was dying for some time, but that helps little when the moment actually comes. It had been the closest of marriages, and she had been his strength. Now, quite suddenly, she was no longer needed, and she was alone. She was only fifty-two. The years must have stretched ahead endlessly.

The funeral of George VI was one of the great outpourings of national grief. His coffin was brought from Sandringham to London, just like his father's before

Winston Churchill, the Prime Minister, and other ministers waiting as their new young Queen comes down the steps of the BOAC plane which brought her home after her father's sudden death.

ABOVE: George VI's funeral procession 23rd February 1952. Mourning crowds lined the whole route from Westminster to Paddington Station where the coffin was put on the train to Windsor.

RIGHT: The three Queens, all in black with black veils, stand in Westminster Hall at George VI's Lying-in-State. Queen Mary's only consolation might have been that her granddaughter beside her would make a very fitting successor to her father.

him. Even in death, it seems, Albert was doing as his father did, and as his father would have wished. As the train carrying his coffin made its way slowly through the East Anglian countryside to London, it billowed out great clouds of steam. All along the track stood George VI's subjects, doffing their hats and caps in tribute to a beloved King.

Mourners queued for four hours to pay their last respects at the lying-in-state in Westminster Hall. They stood three and four deep, all along the Embankment, over Lambeth Bridge, and far along the Embankment on the other side. Once inside Westminster Hall, they walked slowly and quietly past the coffin, many of them crying. For them, it was a personal loss. On the eve of the funeral, few noticed a slight figure in black and a black veil standing quietly in a doorway. It must have been a real solace to Elizabeth to see the love her father had inspired in so many of his subjects who filed quietly past. Perhaps she thought about her childhood, happy times at Royal Lodge with games of cards and bicycle rides. Times when the four of them were just the four of them and life seemed safe and easy. The following day, as George VI's coffin was lowered into the earth at Windsor, three figures in black veils (the mother and her two daughters) stood by like three women from a Greek Chorus. And the whole country stood still for two minutes' silence.

Monarchy marks the pages of a nation's history. One King dies, and another is born. The page is turned and a new era begins. On 5th May, just three months after George VI's funeral, the first meeting of the Coronation Commission took place with Prince Philip in the chair. Tim Heald records that Prince Philip got to work at once, not bothering with niceties or preliminaries. 'My Lords and Gentlemen,' he said. 'First, as Chairman, welcome to the Coronation Commission. There is a tremendous amount of work to be done, so the sooner we get down to it the better.' It was typical of the Prince – direct and full of energy. And of course he was right, there was a tremendous amount to be done because Coronations take a great deal of doing.

But at the same time, Prince Philip was having to get used to the new order of things. As he told his biographer Basil Boothroyd in 1970, everything changed the day his wife became Queen. 'Within the house, and whatever we did, it was together,' he said of the times before that fateful day. 'I suppose I naturally filled the principal position. People used to come to me and ask me what to do. In 1952 the whole thing changed, very, very considerably.' In fact, nothing was done, however large or small, without asking the Queen.

Prince Philip, the Queen and their two children, plus their entire retinue and Bobo and John Dean and the children's nanny, had by now moved back in to Buckingham Palace. They had tried to hold out at Clarence House, their own

Elizabeth and her family in September 1952 at Balmoral – the last summer before she was crowned Queen. These breaks in Scotland were especially enjoyed.

LEFT: Summer 1952 at Balmoral. Elizabeth II looks forward confidently to a reign for which she had been well prepared and trained. RIGHT: The young Queen together with the heir to the throne, Prince Charles, aged three-and-a-half.

home, but precedence, as ever, prevailed. Back they went behind the railings. For the Queen, there must have been renewed memories of that first time she moved to the Palace, aged ten, leaving behind the relaxed informality of 145 Piccadilly. For Prince Philip, it must have felt a bit like going to prison. Queen Elizabeth, now the Queen Mother, and Princess Margaret moved out to Clarence House.

Queen Mary, now nearly eighty-five, remained at Marlborough House, half way between Buckingham Palace and Clarence House. To her friend, Osbert Sitwell, she wrote: 'I am beginning to lose my memory, but I mean to get it BACK.' To others she made it clear that, should she die before her granddaughter's Coronation, mourning was on no account to cause a delay to the event. All her life had been dedicated to the Crown, and her death was certainly not going to impede it.

On 26th May it was her birthday. 'Nice fine day, not so hot,' she recorded in her diary. 'My 85th birthday! spent a hectic morning with endless presents arriving and lots of flowers – Mary [her daughter] kindly came at 12 & helped me & we had lunch & tea together – Between 2.30 and 4.30 a number of my family came to see me, very nice of them – hundreds of letters, cards etc. arrived – we tried to deal with them – I felt very much spoilt & had a nice day in spite of my great age.' In May Queen Mary went to Kensington Palace to inspect the details of Queen Victoria's Coronation robes with a view to possibly making reference to them in Elizabeth's robes. In the summer, she spent some weeks at Sandringham, as she did at Christmas, although then she spent most of the time in her own room. In February, she went to inspect the stands being erected along the Coronation route. On 24th March 1953, Queen Mary died, peacefully, in her own home.

All through 1952, Queen Elizabeth was preparing for her Coronation, and performing for the first time those rituals of monarchy which would mark the unfolding of each year for the rest of her life. In June, she rode alone at the Trooping the Colour for the first time. In November, it was the State Opening of Parliament. At Christmas, from Sandringham, she made her first Christmas broadcast to the nation and the Commonwealth. 'Pray for me on that day,' she said, looking forward to the Coronation. 'Pray that God may give me wisdom and strength to carry out the solemn promises I shall be making.'

Queen Elizabeth II making her first Christmas broadcast to listeners all over the world in 1952.

ABOVE: Queen Elizabeth in the carriage going to her first State Opening of Parliament in 1952 and (RIGHT) at the ceremony in 1995.

The young Queen threw herself into her work. During that first year before the Coronation she attended more than 450 public engagements. Having shown little interest in matters of state before her Accession, she now wanted to know everything and everyone. Winston Churchill, who had wept openly when King George VI died, and who was apprehensive at having to deal with such a young Queen, found her mature for her years, very matter of fact, and extremely industrious. Moreover, they had fun together. Soon the Prime Minister's Tuesday evening sessions at Buckingham Palace were lasting longer and longer.

All the time, preparations for the Coronation were moving ahead. The Duke of Norfolk, as Earl Marshal and overall organiser, wanted to know whether the Coronation robes could be trimmed in rabbit fur rather than ermine, these still being hard economic times following the war. The answer was yes. Sir Norman Hartnell, who was designing the Coronation gown, submitted nine designs in all. The selected gown was embroidered with the floral emblems of the four parts of the United Kingdom, with Commonwealth national flowers round the hem. In the ballroom at Buckingham Palace, the Queen and her attendants paced up and down, practising for the long walk into Westminster Abbey and up the nave — they used white sheets pinned together to give them some idea of the extent of the Coronation train. If Philip got bored and played the fool a bit, she told him not to be silly and started all over again.

Along the Coronation route, stalls and barriers were erected. The seating plan in Westminster Abbey was rearranged many times, pleasing most and offending a few. Music was composed. The anointing oil was made up by a chemist in Bond Street, using the same amounts of musk and jasmine and orange flowers as for the Coronation of Charles I. Dukes and Duchesses were instructed on matters of attire and etiquette. Labour MPs complained at the cost. Lights were placed in the golden State Coach so that the Queen could be seen by everyone.

Seven hours of television coverage were meticulously planned. To many people's amazement, the Queen was allowing live television coverage inside the Abbey. 300 million people across the world would watch the ceremony and in Britain, thousands bought their first television set. Newspapers churned out facts and figures and Coronation anecdotes. Tents went up in the London parks to house the 60000 troops who would line the Coronation route. The Post Office installed 3280 extra telephone lines to cater for all the foreign commentators. Heads of

Queen Elizabeth II and Prince Philip – a formal photograph to mark the year of her Coronation.

State arrived from the four corners of the Commonwealth. London hotels were booked up months ahead. Coronation plates and mugs and tea towels flooded the shops. Flags and banners were ready to be waved across the land. Street parties were planned. A day of holiday was announced. School children everywhere waited to cheer. Coronation fever was at a pitch.

Coronation Day dawned on 2nd June 1953. It had rained during the night, and now there was a fine drizzle. Outside Buckingham Palace, people were sitting around their primus stoves, wrapped in blankets and plastic macs against the chill, making their breakfasts. 30 000 people had camped out in the rain, spending most of the night singing and talking and generally having a good time. As on the eve of the Coronation of George VI, it must have been difficult to get a good night's sleep in Buckingham Palace. As Princess Elizabeth, aged eleven, had bounded out of bed at 5 am to have a peep at the crowds outside, so Queen Elizabeth, aged twenty-seven, must have done the same. By the end of the day, some 850000 people had flocked to the centre of London to have a share of the great day.

As the golden State Coach emerged from Buckingham Palace at 11 am bearing their young and smiling Queen, all lit up by the specially-installed lights and wearing a glittering tiara, the crowds went wild. Inside the Abbey, hushed and solemn, she spoke her vows in her clear, steady voice. The Archbishop of Canterbury raised the heavily bejewelled St Edward's Crown high and then placed it on her young head. Prince Philip came forward in his Coronation robes, mounted the steps to the Queen's throne, knelt and spoke these words: 'I Philip, Duke of Edinburgh, do become your liegeman of life and limb and of earthly worship; and faith and truth I will bear unto you, to live and die against all manner of folks.' His mother Princess Alice, in her grey nun's habit, watched as Elizabeth took Philip's hand in hers before he stooped to touch the Crown and kiss his Queen. Queen of 650 million people throughout Britain and the Commonwealth.

Back at the Palace, Queen Elizabeth II and Prince Philip, their two young children, Charles and Anne, Queen Elizabeth the Queen Mother and Princess Margaret came out onto the balcony to acknowledge the cheering crowds below who pressed against the railings and stretched away into the distance as far as the eye could see. Queen Elizabeth and Prince Philip came out six times in all, the last being at midnight.

Inside Westminster Abbey, 2nd June 1953. 'Pray for me on that day.' Queen Elizabeth had said in her first Christmas broadcast. 'Pray that God may give me wisdom and strength to carry out the solemn promises I shall be making'.

What did they think as they smiled and waved? What mixture of happiness, pride and dread did Philip feel? And what memories did Elizabeth have of that other Coronation Day, her father's, all those years ago when she was just eleven and stood there on that same spot, smiling and waving, looking down in amazement at the sea of faces, that ocean of affection and high expectation spread out below?

★   ★   ★

This year the Queen is seventy. She was just twenty-six when her father died and she inherited the throne – twenty-seven on the day of her Coronation.

George VI died young, at fifty-seven, so at twenty-six Princess Elizabeth was an unusually young monarch. And yet, by all accounts, when the moment came she was ready. Trained by her father in the day-to-day business of monarchy, and sharing his profoundly held beliefs about the importance of the role, she took over

LEFT ABOVE AND BELOW: Balcony scenes at Buckingham Palace on Coronation Day, the stage on which all the major scenes of monarchy are played.
BELOW: A typical street party for the Coronation with flags, bunting, jelly for the children, singing and dancing. A good time had by all.

where he left off with relative ease. When asked about certain duties she was often known to have replied: 'Did my father do that? Then so shall I.'

Today, forty-four years on, Elizabeth is still performing the tasks and rituals of monarchy which she learnt and promised faithfully to undertake all those years ago. Since that time there have been many changes, both in society at large and in its attitude towards the monarchy, many ups and downs and occasions when it seemed that it was becoming less popular than it had been in her father's day. But the Queen herself has never lost the country's respect. Opening Parliament, receiving foreign dignitaries, inspecting regiments, taking parades, unveiling plaques, and visiting institutions up and down the country, she brings to the job the same serious dedication that she did on her twenty-first birthday in 1947 when she said; 'I declare before you all that my whole life, whether it be long or short, shall be devoted to your service . . .'.

BELOW: The Queen on a walkabout on Maundy Thursday after distributing Maundy Money at the traditional service held in 1995 at Coventry Cathedral.
RIGHT: The Queen visits Birds Eye Walls' ice cream factory, Gloucester 1995.

ABOVE: Trooping the Colour, the Queen's official birthday, 1995.

RIGHT: Britain's Queen Mother and Queen with officers of the Irish
Guards on St Patrick's Day 1995.

BIBLIOGRAPHY

Airlie, Mabell, Countess of *Thatched with Gold*, Hutchinson, 1962

Bradford, Sarah *George VI*, Fontana, 1991

Piers Brendon and Phillip Whitehead *The Windsors A Dynasty Revealed*, Hodder & Stoughton, 1994

Boothroyd, Basil *Philip: An Informal Biography*, Longman, 1971

Channon, Sir Henry *Chips: The Diaries of Sir Henry Channon*, Weidenfeld & Nicolson, 1967

Cooper, Diana *The Light of Common Day*, Rupert Hart-Davis, 1959

Crawford, Marion *The Little Princesses*, Cassell, 1950

Heald, Tim *The Duke: A Portrait of Prince Philip*, Hodder & Stoughton, 1991

Douglas Keay *Elizabeth II: Portrait of a Monarch*, Century, 1991

Lacey, Robert *Majesty: Elizabeth II and the House of Windsor*, Hutchinson, 1977

Longford, Elizabeth Countess of, *The Royal House of Windsor*, Weidenfeld and Nicolson, 1974

Longford, Elizabeth Countess of, *Elizabeth R*, Weidenfeld & Nicolson, 1983

Morrah, Dermot *To be a King*, Hutchinson, 1968

Nicolson, Harold *King George V (His Life and Reign)*, Constable, 1952

Parker, John *The Queen*, Headline, 1991

Parker, John *Prince Philip, A Critical Biography*, Sidgwick and Jackson, 1990

Pope-Hennessey, James *Queen Mary 1867–1953*, Allen & Unwin, an imprint of HarperCollins, 1959

Wheeler-Bennett, Sir John W *King George VI, His Life & Reign*, Macmillan, 1958

Windsor, HRH the Duke of *A King's Story*, Cassell, 1951

Ziegler, Philip *King Edward VIII, the Official Biography*, Collins, 1990

INDEX

Page numbers in bold denote illustrations.
Page numbers in italic denote captions.